THE DIARY
of
DR. JOHN WILLIAM POLIDORI

1816

RELATING TO BYRON, SHELLEY, ETC.
EDITED AND ELUCIDATED BY
WILLIAM MICHAEL ROSSETTI

First published in 1911

This edition published by Read Books Ltd.
Copyright © 2019 Read Books Ltd.
This book is copyright and may not be
reproduced or copied in any way without
the express permission of the publisher in writing

British Library Cataloguing-in-Publication Data
A catalogue record for this book is available
from the British Library

CONTENTS

JOHN WILLIAM POLIDORI

John William Polidori was born in London, England in 1795. In 1810, he enrolled at the University of Edinburgh, where he wrote a thesis on sleepwalking and graduated as a doctor of medicine. In 1816, Polidori entered Lord Byron's service as his personal physician, accompanying him through Europe and keeping a diary of their travels.

While at Byron's villa beside Lake Geneva, in Switzerland, they were joined by Percy Bysshe Shelley and Mary Shelley. Storms and tumultuous weather confined them to the indoors, where they and Byron's assorted other guests took to reading to each other from a book of ghost stories. One evening, Byron challenged all his guests to write one themselves. The guests obliged, and Polidori wrote *The Vampyre*.

After parting ways with Byron, he travelled through Italy before returning to England, and in April of 1819, his story 'The Vampyre' was published in *New Monthly Magazine*. The story is now seen as a progenitor of the romantic vampire genre of fantasy fiction, and the first modern vampire story ever published in English. Suffering from depression and gambling debts, Polidori died two years after its appearance, possibly via suicide, aged just 25.

"Mi fur mostrati gli spiriti magni
Che del vederli in me stesso n'esalto."

—Dante.

DEDICATED

TO MY TWO DAUGHTERS

HELEN AND MARY

WHO WITH MY
LITTLE GRAND-DAUGHTER IMOGENE
KEEP THE HOME OF MY CLOSING YEARS
STILL IN GOOD CHEER

THE DIARY
of
DR. JOHN WILLIAM POLIDORI

INTRODUCTION

A person whose name finds mention in the books about Byron, and to some extent in those about Shelley, was John William Polidori, M.D.; he was Lord Byron's travelling physician in 1816, when his Lordship quitted England soon after the separation from his wife. I, who now act as Editor of his Diary, am a nephew of his, born after his death. Dr. Polidori figures not very advantageously in the books concerning Byron and Shelley. He is exhibited as overweening and petulant, too fond of putting himself forward face to face with those two heroes of our poetical literature, and too touchy when either of them declined to take him at his own estimation. I will allow that this judgment of Polidori is, so far as it goes, substantially just; and that some of the recorded anecdotes of him prove him deficient in self-knowledge, lacking prudence and reserve, and ignoring the distinction between a dignified and a quarrelsome attitude of mind. He was, in fact, extremely young when he went abroad in April 1816 with Byron, to whom he had been recommended by Sir Henry Halford; he was then only twenty years of age (born on September 7, 1795), Byron being twenty-eight, and Shelley twenty-three. The recommendation given to so very young a man is a little surprising. It would be a mistake, however, to suppose that Polidori was without some solid attainments, and some considerable share of talent. He was the son of Gaetano Polidori, a Tuscan man of letters who, after being secretary to the celebrated dramatist Alfieri, had settled in London as a teacher of Italian, and of his English wife, a Miss Pierce; the parents (my maternal grand-parents) survived to a great age, only dying in 1853. John Polidori, after receiving his education in the Roman Catholic College of Ampleforth (Yorkshire), studied medicine in Edinburgh, and took his doctor's degree at a singularly early age—I believe almost unexampled—the age of nineteen. His ambition was fully as much for literary as for professional distinction; and he published, besides *The Vampyre* to which I shall have to recur, a prose tale named *Ernestus Berchtold*, a volume of verse containing a drama entitled *Ximenes*, and some other writings.

One of these writings is the text to a volume, published in 1821, entitled *Sketches Illustrative of the Manners and Costumes of France, Switzerland, and Italy*, by R. Bridgens. The name of Polidori is not indeed recorded in this book, but I know as a certainty that he was the writer. One of the designs in the volume shows the costume of women at Lerici just about the time when Shelley was staying there, in the closing months of his life, and a noticeable costume it was. Polidori himself—though I am not aware that he ever received any instruction in drawing worth speaking of—had some considerable native gift in sketching faces and figures with lifelike expression; I possess a few examples to prove as much. The Diary shows that he took some serious and intelligent interest in works of art, as well as in literature; and he was clearly a rapid and somewhat caustic judge of character—perhaps a correct one. He was a fine, rather romantic-looking young man, as evidenced by his portrait in the National Portrait Gallery, accepted from me by that Institution in 1895.

Dr. Polidori's life was a short one. Not long after quitting Lord Byron in 1816 he returned to London, and in Norwich continued his medical career, but eventually relinquished this, and began studying for the Bar. It is said that Miss Harriett Martineau was rather in love with him in Norwich. In August 1821 he committed suicide with poison—having, through losses in gambling, incurred a debt of honour which he had no present means of clearing off. That he did take poison, prussic acid, was a fact perfectly well known in his family; but it is curious to note that the easy-going and good-naturedly disposed coroner's jury were content to return a verdict without eliciting any distinct evidence as to the cause of death, and they simply pronounced that he had "died by the visitation of God."

The matter was reported in two papers, *The Traveller* and *The New Times*. I possess a copy, made by my mother at the time, of the reports; and it may perhaps be as well inserted here.

COPIED FROM *THE TRAVELLER*.

Monday Evening [*August 27th, 1821*].

Melancholy Event.—Mr. Polidori, residing in Great Pulteney Street, retired to rest about his usual time on Thursday night; the servant, not finding him rise at the usual hour yesterday, went to his room between eleven and twelve o'clock, and found him groaning, and apparently in the last agonies of death. An alarm was given and medical aid was immediately called, but before the arrival of Surgeons Copeland and Davies, he was no more. His father was at the time on his journey to London to see his son, and arrived about three hours after the event. We understand the deceased was about twenty-six years of age, and had for some time accompanied Lord Byron in Italy. A Coroner's Inquest will sit this day to ascertain the cause of his death.

THE DIARY OF
DR. JOHN WILLIAM POLIDORI

COPIED FROM THE NEW TIMES.

Tuesday [*September 11th, 1821*].

Coroner's Inquest on John Polidori, Esquire.—An Inquisition has been taken before T. Higgs, Esquire, Deputy Coroner, at the residence of the father of the above unfortunate gentleman, in Great Pulteney Street, Golden Square, who was discovered lying on his bed in a state nearly approaching to death, and soon afterwards expired.

Charlotte Reed, the servant to Mr. Gaetano Polidori, the father of the deceased, said her master's son lived in the house, and for some time had been indisposed. On Monday the 20th of August last he returned from Brighton, since which his conduct manifested strong symptoms of incoherence, and he gave his order for dinner in a very strange manner. On the Thursday following the deceased dined with a gentleman residing in the same house, and on that occasion he appeared very much depressed in his spirits. About nine o'clock the same evening he ordered witness to leave a glass (tumbler) in his room; this was unusual, but one was placed as he desired. Deceased told her he was unwell; if therefore he did not get up by twelve o'clock the next day, not to disturb him. Witness, however, a few minutes before twelve, went into his room to open the shutters, and on her return saw the deceased lying in bed; he was not in any unusual position, but seemed extremely ill. Witness immediately left the room, went upstairs, and communicated what she had observed to a gentleman, who instantly came down. Witness then went for medical assistance. The deceased was about twenty-six years of age.—Mr. John Deagostini, the gentleman alluded to by the last witness, corroborated her statement on his giving him the invitation to dine, which he accepted in a way quite different from his usual conduct. Witness also observed that, some time since, the deceased had met with an accident—was thrown out of his gig, and seriously hurt in the head. On Thursday at dinner he spoke in half sentences; the conversation was on politics and a future state. The deceased observed rather harshly that witness would see more than him; he appeared to be deranged in his mind, and his countenance was haggard. At dinner he ate very little: soon after left the room, but joined again at tea; hardly spoke a word, and retired at nine o'clock. After breakfast next morning, witness inquired of the servant whether Mr. Polidori had gone out. She replied no, and that he had desired her not to disturb him. About twelve o'clock the servant came to him very much alarmed. Witness went immediately to the apartment of the deceased, and observed a tumbler on the chair, which contained nothing but water, and did not perceive any deleterious substance that the deceased might have taken; he was senseless, and apparently in a dying state.—Mr. Thomas Copeland, a surgeon residing in Golden Square, was sent for suddenly to attend the deceased, and attempted to discharge the contents of the stomach without effect. He lingered for about ten minutes, and expired. Another medical gentleman soon after arrived, but his assistance was also unavailing.—There being no further evidence adduced to prove how the deceased came to his death, the jury, under these circumstances, returned a verdict of—Died by the visitation of God.

Medwin, in his *Conversations with Lord Byron*, gives the following account of how the poet received the news of Dr. Polidori's death. "I was convinced" (said Byron) "something very unpleasant hung over me last night: I expected to hear that somebody I knew was dead. So it turns out—poor Polidori is gone. When he was my physician he was always talking of prussic acid, oil of amber, blowing into veins, suffocating by charcoal, and compounding poisons; but for a different purpose to what the Pontic monarch did, for he has prescribed a dose for himself that would have killed fifty Mithridates—a dose whose effect, Murray says, was so instantaneous that he went off without a spasm or struggle. It seems that disappointment was the cause of this rash act."—The evidence of the servant at the inquest shows that death did not come so very suddenly; and in my own family I always heard the poison spoken of as simply prussic acid.

This is all that I need say at present to explain who Dr. Polidori was; but I must add a few words regarding his Diary.

The day when the young doctor obtained the post of travelling physician to the famous poet and man of fashion, Lord Byron, about to leave England for the Continent, must, no doubt, have been regarded by him and by some of his family as a supremely auspicious one, although in fact it turned out the reverse. The article on Polidori written in *The Dictionary of National Biography* by my valued friend, the late Dr. Garnett, speaks of him as "physician and *secretary* to Lord Byron"; but I never heard that he undertook or performed any secretarial work worth speaking of, and I decidedly believe that he did not. The same statement occurs in the inscription on his likeness in the National Portrait Gallery. Polidori's father had foreseen, in the Byronic scheme, disappointment as only too likely, and he opposed the project, but without success. To be the daily companion and intimate of so great a man as Byron, to visit foreign scenes in his society, to travel into his own father's native land, which he regarded with a feeling of enthusiasm, and with whose language he was naturally well acquainted, to be thus launched upon a career promising the utmost development and satisfaction to his literary as well as professional enterprise—all this may have seemed like the realization of a dream almost too good to be true. To crown all, Mr. Murray, Byron's publisher, had offered Polidori no less a sum than £500 (or 500 guineas) for an account of his forthcoming tour. Polidori therefore began to keep a Diary, heading it *Journal of a Journey through Flanders etc., from April 24, 1816, to_____*; and the blank was eventually filled in with the date "December 28, 1816"; it should rather stand "December 30." Portions of the Diary are written with some detail, and a perceptible aim at literary effect—Murray's £500 being manifestly in view; in other instances the jottings are slight, and merely enough for guiding the memory. On this footing the Journal goes on up to June 30,

1816. It was then dropped, as Polidori notes "through neglect and dissipation," for he saw a great deal of company. On September 5 he wrote up some summarized reminiscences; and from September 16, the day when he parted company with Byron at Cologny, near Geneva, and proceeded to journey through Italy on his own account, he continued with some regularity up to December 30, when he was sojourning in Pisa. That is the latest day of which any record remains; but it is known from other evidence that Dr. Polidori continued in Italy up to April 14, 1817: he then left Venice in company with the new Earl of Guilford and his mother—being their travelling physician. Whether the Journal is in any fair degree interesting or brightly written is a question which the reader will settle for himself; as a document relevant to the life of two illustrious poets, it certainly merits some degree of attention.

My own first acquaintance with the Diary of Dr. Polidori dates back to 1869, when I was preparing the Memoir of Shelley which preludes my edition of his poems, published in 1870; I then availed myself of the Shelleian information contained in the Diary, and even gave two or three verbatim extracts from it. The MS. book was at that time the property of a sister of his, Miss Charlotte Lydia Polidori, a lady of advanced age. I regret to say that my aunt, on receiving the MS. back from me, took it into her head to read it through—a thing which I fancy she had never before done, or certainly had not done for very many years, and that she found in it some few passages which she held to be "improper," and, with the severe virtue so characteristic of an English maiden aunt, she determined that those passages should no longer exist. I can remember one about Byron and a chambermaid at Ostend, and another, later on, about Polidori himself. My aunt therefore took the trouble of copying out the whole Diary, minus the peccant passages, and she then ruthlessly destroyed the original MS. After her death—which occurred in January 1890, when she had attained the age of eighty-seven years—her transcript came into my possession. Its authority is only a shade less safe than that of the original, and it is from the transcript that I have had to work in compiling my present volume.

I will now refer in some detail to the matter of Dr. Polidori's romantic tale, *The Vampyre*; not only because this matter is of some literary interest in itself, but more especially because the account of it given in *The Dictionary of National Biography* treats Polidori, in this regard, with no indulgence, and I believe (however unintentionally on the part of the late Dr. Garnett) with less than justice. He says: "In April 1819 he [Polidori] published in *The New Monthly Magazine*, and also in pamphlet-form, the celebrated story of *The Vampyre*, which he attributed to Byron. The ascription was fictitious. Byron had in fact, in June 1816, begun to write at Geneva a story with this title, in emulation of Mrs. Shelley's *Frankenstein*; but dropped it before reaching the superstition which it was to have illustrated. He sent the fragment to Murray upon the appearance of Polidori's fabrication, and it is inserted in his works. He further protested in a carelessly good-natured disclaimer addressed to *Galignani's Messenger*."

The facts of the case appear to be as follows. As we shall see in the Diary, Polidori began, near Geneva, a tale which (according to Mrs. Shelley) was about a "skull-headed lady," and he was clearly aware that Byron had commenced a story about a vampyre. After quitting Byron, Polidori, in conversation with the Countess of Breuss, mentioned in his Journal, spoke (unless we are to discredit his own account) of the subject of the great poet's tale; the Countess questioned whether anything could be made of such a theme, and Polidori then tried his hand at carrying it out. He left the MS. with the Countess, and thought little or no more about it. After his departure from that neighbourhood some person who was travelling there (one might perhaps infer a lady) obtained the MS. either from the Countess of Breuss or from some person acquainted with the Countess: this would, I suppose, be the Madame Gatelier who is named in the Journal along with the Countess. The traveller then forwarded the tale to the Publisher, Colburn, telling him—and this statement was printed by Colburn as an *Extract of a Letter from Geneva*—that certain tales were "undertaken by Lord B[yron], the physician [Polidori], and Miss M. W. Godwin," and that the writer received from her female friend "the outline of each of these stories." She did not say that the completed *Vampyre* was the production of Byron; but Colburn inferred this, and in the magazine he attributed it to Byron, printing his name as author.

Among the papers which were left by Dr. Polidori at the time of his death, and which have come into my possession, are the drafts of two letters of his—one addressed to Mr. Henry Colburn, and the other to the Editor of *The Morning Chronicle*. These letters were actually dispatched, and (having no sort of reason to suspect the contrary) I assume that they contain a truthful account of the facts. If so, they exonerate Polidori from the imputation of having planned or connived at a literary imposture. In his letter to Mr. Colburn he affirms (as will be seen) that the following incidents in his tale were borrowed from Byron's project: the departure of two friends from England, one of them dying in Greece [but it is in fact near Ephesus] after exacting from his companion an oath not to mention his death; the revival of the dead man, and his then making love to the sister of his late companion. The story begun by Byron and published along with *Mazeppa* contains the incidents above named, except only the important incident of the dead man's revival and his subsequent love-making. Byron's extant writing, which is a mere fragment, affords no trace of that upshot; but Polidori must have known that such was the intended sequel. It may be added that the resemblance between these productions of Byron and of Polidori extends only to incidents: the form of narrative is different.

I proceed to give the letter of Dr. Polidori to Mr. Colburn, followed by the letter to the Editor of *The Morning Chronicle*. This latter goes over a good deal of the same ground as the letter to Colburn, so I shorten it very considerably.

THE DIARY OF
DR. JOHN WILLIAM POLIDORI

JOHN POLIDORI TO HENRY COLBURN.

[London], *April 2* (1819).

SIR,

I received a copy of the magazine of last April (the present month), and am sorry to find that your Genevan correspondent has led you into a mistake with regard to the tale of *The Vampyre*—which is *not* Lord Byron's, but was written *entirely* by me at the request of a lady, who (upon my mentioning that his Lordship had said that it was his intention of writing a ghost story, depending for interest upon the circumstances of two friends leaving England, and one dying in Greece, the other finding him alive, upon his return, and making love to his sister) saying that she thought it impossible to work up such materials, desired I would write it for her, which I did in two idle mornings by her side. These circumstances above mentioned, and the one of the dying man having obtained an oath that the survivor should not in any way disclose his decease, are the only parts of the tale belonging to his Lordship. I desire, therefore, that you will positively contradict your statement in the next number, by the insertion of this note.

With regard to my own tale, it is imperfect and unfinished. I had rather therefore it should not appear in the magazine; and, if the Editor had sent his communication, as he mentions, he would have been spared this mistake.

But, sir, there is one circumstance of which I must request a further explanation. I observe upon the back of your publication the announcement of a separate edition. Now, upon buying this, I find that it states in the title-page that it was entered into Stationers' Hall upon March 27, consequently before your magazine was published. I wish therefore to ask for information how this tale passed from the hands of your Editor into those of a publisher.

As it is a mere trifle, I should have had no objection to its

18

appearing in your magazine, as I could, in common with any other, have extracted it thence, and republished it. But I shall not sit patiently by and see it taken without my consent, and appropriated by any person. As therefore it must have passed through your hands (as stated in the magazine) from a correspondent, I shall expect that you will account to me for the publishers, Messrs. Sherwood and Neely, having possession of it and appropriating it to themselves; and demand either that a compensation be made me, or that its separate publication be instantly suppressed.

Hoping for an immediate answer, which will save me the trouble of obtaining an injunction, I remain,

Sir,

Your obedient servant,
JOHN POLIDORI.

TO THE EDITOR OF *THE MORNING CHRONICLE*.

SIR,

As you were the first person to whom I wrote to state that the tale of *The Vampyre* was not Lord Byron's, I beg you to insert the following statement in your paper.... The tale, as I stated to you in my letter, was written upon the foundation of a purposed and begun story of Lord Byron's.... Lord Byron, in a letter dated Venice, stated that he knew nothing of the Vampyre story, and hated vampyres; but, while this letter was busily circulating in all the London and provincial papers, the fragment at the end of *Mazeppa* was in the hands of his publishers in Albemarle Street, with the date of June 17, 1816, attached to it, being the beginning of his tale upon this very foundation. My development was written on the Continent, and left with a lady at whose request it was undertaken; in the course of three mornings by her side it was produced, and left with her. From her hands, by means of a correspondent, without my knowledge, it came into those of the Editor of *The New Monthly*, with a letter stating it to be an *ébauche* of Lord Byron's. Mr. Watts, as Editor of that magazine, stated in *his* notice that the tale which accompanies the letters "we also present to our readers without pledging ourselves for its authenticity as the production of Lord Byron"; and he continues, "We should suppose it to have been committed to paper rather from the recital of a third person." This, however, after the publication of 700 copies, was cancelled by the *publisher*, and another notice inserted stating it to be decidedly his Lordship's, in direct opposition (as I am informed) to the Editor's will—who has since retired from the conduct of the magazine.

Immediately it was published I procured a copy; and, upon finding that it was an almost forgotten trifle of my own, instantly wrote to you as Editor of *The Morning Chronicle*, stating the little share Lord Byron had in the work. This was upon the Friday evening after its publication. I at the same time wrote to the publishers of the tale in its separate form, and to those of the magazine, to stop its sale under his Lordship's name. On Monday the publishers of the magazine called upon me, and promised it should be instantly announced as mine.... When I came to claim my share in the profits, I was offered £30, instead of nearly £300....

Your obedient servant,

JOHN POLIDORI.

* * * * *

The prefatory note to *The Vampyre*, in *The New Monthly Magazine*, runs thus: "We received several private letters in the course of last autumn from a friend travelling on the Continent, and among others the following, which we give to the public on account of its containing anecdotes of an individual concerning whom the most trifling circumstances, if they tend to mark even the minor features of his mind, cannot fail of being considered important and valuable by those who know how to appreciate his erratic but transcendent genius. The tale which accompanied the letter we have also much pleasure in presenting to our readers.— Ed." There is also a final note thus: "We have in our possession the tale of Dr. ——, as well as the outline of that of Miss Godwin. The latter has already appeared under the title of *Frankenstein, or The Modern Prometheus*. The former, however, upon consulting with its author, we may probably hereafter give to our readers.—Ed."

Two questions arise as to that prefatory note: (1) Did the Editor really write it, or did the Publisher Colburn write it? (2) Is the averment true or false that the Editor (or the Publisher) had received in the course of the preceding autumn "several private letters" from the same person who had now forwarded a letter enclosing *The Vampyre*?

Murray wrote to Lord Byron on April 27, 1819. He speaks of the publication of *The Vampyre* in *The New Monthly Magazine*, and afterwards in book-form, and proceeds: "The Editor of that journal has quarrelled with the Publisher, and has called this morning to exculpate himself from the baseness of the transaction. He says that he received it from Dr. Polidori for a small sum; Polidori averring that the whole plan of it was yours, and that it was merely written out by him. The Editor inserted it with a short statement to this effect; but, to his astonishment, Colburn cancelled the leaf.... He informs me that Polidori, finding that the sale exceeded his expectation and that he had sold it too cheap, went to the Editor and declared that he would deny it."

This statement by Murray makes it probable that the paragraph purporting to come from the Editor, or some substantial part of it, really emanated from the Publisher, and the same is definitely asserted in Polidori's letter to *The Morning Chronicle*; but Murray's letter does not settle the question whether the allegation about a traveller at Geneva was true or false. The Editor's assertion that "he received it from Dr. Polidori for a small sum" does not by any means clear up all the facts. It seems quite possible that there really was a correspondent at Geneva who sent to the Editor the MS. of *The Vampyre*, along with that of Polidori's other tale, and an outline of Mary Shelley's *Frankenstein*, as expressly affirmed in the final note signed "Ed."; and that the Editor, having no right to publish *The Vampyre* unless by authority of its writer, spoke to Polidori about it. How could Polidori dispose of it "for a small sum" if he alleged that it was written by Byron, or by any one other than himself? He averred "that the whole plan of it was" Byron's—and this is apparently true; adding "that it was merely written out by" himself—in the sense not of having written from Byron's dictation, but of having composed a story founded upon Byron's intended incidents. Murray's final phrase—that Polidori "went to the Editor, and declared that he would deny it"—is loosely expressed, but seems to mean that he would deny Byron's authorship of *The Vampyre*—and so in fact he did.

If we suppose (as did Murray apparently) that Polidori had in the first instance planned a deliberate imposture, and had palmed off upon the Editor *The Vampyre* as being virtually the writing of Byron, we are encountered by three difficulties left unexplained: (1) What plea could Polidori advance for having the MS. and the right of publishing it? (2) Why did he sell for "a *small* sum" a work which, if written by the world-famous Lord Byron, would be worth a very considerable sum? (3) Why did the Editor pay to Polidori a sum, whether small or large, for a book which, according to this assumption, was avowedly not the writing of himself, but the writing and property of Byron? All these difficulties are avoided, and no other serious difficulties arise, if we assume that the account given by Polidori is the true one, viz. that he offered the tale to the Editor as being his own composition, strictly modelled upon a series of incidents invented by Byron.

Polidori's letter, addressed to the Editor of *The Morning*

Chronicle, was, as I have already said, delivered to the office of that paper. It was not however published there, as Messrs. Sherwood, Neely, and Jones, the publishers of *The Vampyre* in its book-form, represented to Polidori that the appearance of such a letter would tend to compromise them, and he therefore, out of consideration for this firm, withdrew the letter unprinted. This is Polidori's own statement, contained in the Introduction to another romantic tale of his, *Ernestus Berchtold*, published in 1819; being the tale by Polidori which, as stated by the Editor of *The New Monthly Magazine*, had been sent to him along with *The Vampyre* and the outline of *Frankenstein*. Besides all this, the Doctor wrote a brief letter, published in *The Courier* on May 5, 1819, saying—what was clearly the fact—"Though the groundwork is certainly Lord Byron's, its development is mine."

I must now revert for a moment to the "skull-headed lady." In the Introduction above named, Polidori asserts that that tale, *Ernestus Berchtold*, was the one which he began at Cologny. It does not contain any sort of mention of any skull-headed lady. There is some supernatural machinery in the story, of a rather futile kind; it could be excluded without affecting the real basis of the narrative, which relates the love-affair and marriage of a young Swiss patriot with a lady who is ultimately identified as his sister. As to Mrs. Shelley's allegation that the (non-existent) skull-headed lady was punished for "peeping through a keyhole," no such incident exists in *Ernestus Berchtold*; there is, however, a passage where a certain Julia seeks to solve a mystery by looking "through the wainscot of a closet for wood." Her head, after this inspection, remains exactly what it was before.

The Vampyre was in its way a great success. As stated in *The Dictionary of National Biography*, Byron's name gave Polidori's production great celebrity on the Continent, where *The Vampyre* was held to be quite the thing which it behoved Byron to have written. It formed the groundwork of Marschner's opera, and nearly half a volume of Dumas's *Memoirs* is occupied by an account of the representation of a French play founded upon it.

THE DIARY

1816. *April 24.*—I left London at 10 in the morning, with Lord Byron, Scrope Davies, Esq., and J. Hobhouse, Esq.

[Mr. Scrope Berdmore Davies had been one of Byron's fellow-students and intimates at Cambridge University, and had continued familiar with him at Newstead Abbey and elsewhere. He has been described as "no less remarkable for elegance of taste than for a generous high-mindedness." Mr. John Cam Hobhouse (afterwards Sir J. C. Hobhouse, and ultimately Lord Broughton de Gifford) was, it need hardly be said, a peculiarly close friend of Byron. He had accompanied him in his travels in Greece prior to the commencement of *Childe Harold*, wrote notes to that poem, and to the last upheld the essential fineness of his Lordship's character. Byron's intention to travel along with Hobhouse in the spring of 1816 was not a new project conceived in consequence of his separation, only completed on April 22, from his wife. He had entertained this scheme before his daughter Ada was born on December 10, 1815, and had announced it to his wife, to whom the notion was not agreeable.]

The view from Shooter's Hill was extensive and beautiful, being on a much larger scale than the view from Stirling.

[Polidori mentions Stirling, as being no doubt a reminiscence of his own, from the days when he had been in Edinburgh to take his medical degree.]

The plain, enamelled with various colours according to the different growth of the corn, spread far before our sight, was divided irregularly by the river. The Thames next, with its majestic waves, flowed in the plain below, bearing numerous fleets upon its flood. Its banks in many parts were beautiful. The chalky banks were alternated with the swelling hills, rising from the waves, of the pleasing green-brown, the effect of the first dawn of spring on the vegetable creation.

At Canterbury we saw the Cathedral. I know not how it was, whether my mind had been prepared by the previous sight of glorious nature to receive pleasing impressions, but the spot where the high altar and Thomas à Becket's tomb stood seemed to me one of the most beautiful effects that I had ever seen arising from Saxo-Gothic architecture; for, though it had not all the airiness and awe-inspiring height that I had seen in other cathedrals, yet its simple beauty pleased me more than anything I had yet seen.

Remounting, we soon arrived at Dover, where we slept, when the packet-boat captain had sufficiently disturbed us.

April 25.—This day was spent at Dover. The greater part was occupied in procuring what had been neglected in London, and in seeing the carriage well packed up. After dinner, however, we went in search of Churchill's tomb, raised, we had learned, to his memory by his friend Wilkes. Arrived at the house of the sexton, he led us to a ruined church, passing through which we came into a churchyard, where children, heedless and unconscious of what they trampled on, sportively ran amid the raised turf graves. He pointed out to us a tombstone, undistinguished from those of the tradesmen near him, having merely, like them, a square tablet stuck into the ground, whereon was written, "Here lie the remains of the celebrated Churchill.

"Life to the last enjoyed, here Churchill lies.

Candidate."

[By Churchill.] The green turf was beginning already to decay upon his tomb, which when the sexton heard us lamenting he assured us that his grave, as well as the rest, would be newly decked as soon as Nature had vested its fullest green—for that was an old custom. Churchill owed, then, only to a common hand what the pride of a friend refused—the safety of his burial-place. Wilkes only sought the gratification of his vanity. While he consigned his friend's last relics to the keeping of a tablet, he consigned his own pride in such a friend to the keeping of a column in his own grounds. Yet I do not know whether the scene was not more moving, though no vainly pompous inscription pointed out the spot where this poet was buried.

There were two authors; one, the most distinguished of his age; another, whose name is rising rapidly; (and a third, ambitious for literary distinction). What a lesson it was for them when, having asked the sexton if he knew why so many came to see this tomb, he said: "I cannot tell; I had not the burying of him."

[Byron, after settling in the Villa Diodati near Geneva, recorded this same incident in a composition entitled *Churchill's Grave, a Fact Literally Rendered*. He wrote a memorandum to say that in this poem he had intentionally imitated the style of Wordsworth, "its beauties and its defects." The composition therefore is essentially un-Byronic in method, and perhaps Wordsworth would not have recognized in it many of his own "beauties." The lines are as follows—

"I stood beside the grave of him who blazed
The comet of a season, and I saw
The humblest of all sepulchres, and gazed
With not the less of sorrow and of awe
On that neglected turf and quiet stone,
With name no clearer than the names unknown
Which lay unread around it. And I ask'd
The gardener of that ground why it might be
That for this plant strangers his memory task'd,
Through the thick deaths of half a century.
And thus he answered: 'Well, I do not know
Why frequent travellers turn to pilgrims so:
He died before my day of sextonship,
And I had not the digging of this grave.'
And is this all? I thought; and do we rip

The veil of immortality, and crave
I know not what of honour and of light
Through unborn ages, to endure this blight
So soon and so successless? As I said,
The architect of all on which we tread
(For earth is but a tombstone) did essay
To extricate remembrance from the clay
Whose minglings might confuse a Newton's thought,
Were it not that all life must end in one,
Of which we are but dreamers. As he caught
As 'twere the twilight of a former sun,
Thus spoke he: 'I believe the man of whom
You wot, who lies in this selected tomb,
Was a most famous writer in his day;
And therefore travellers step from out their way
To pay him honour;—and myself whate'er
Your honour pleases.' Then most pleased I shook
From out my pocket's avaricious nook
Some certain coins of silver, which (as 'twere
Perforce) I gave this man—though I could spare
So much but inconveniently. Ye smile
(I see ye, ye profane ones, all the while)
Because my homely phrase the truth would tell.
You are the fools, not I; for I did dwell
With a deep thought and with a softened eye
On that old sexton's natural homily,
In which there was obscurity and fame—
The glory and the nothing of a name."

Charles Churchill the satirist, a clergyman who had given up
his standing in the Church, had died in 1764 at Boulogne, aged
only thirty-three. It is clear that his renown was still considerable
in 1816; it is now barely more than a literary reminiscence.]
    We then returned home, where, having delivered my play into
their hands, I had to hear it laughed at—(an author has always a

salvo) partly, I think, from the way in which it was read. One of the party, however—to smoothe, I suppose, my ruffled spirits—took up my play, and apparently read part with great attention, drawing applause from those who before had laughed. He read on with so much attention that the others declared he had never been so attentive before.

[Further on it would appear that this play was named *Cajetan*. I know nothing about it. The name Cajetan is in Italian Gaetano, which was the Christian name of Polidori's father.]

I afterwards went out, and did a very absurd thing, which I told; and found I had not only hurt myself but might possibly hurt others for whom I cared much more.

April 26.—We embarked at 9 o'clock, much hurried, with three servants.

[This means, to judge from a published letter by Byron, 9 o'clock on the evening of April 25. The three servants were Berger (a Swiss), William Fletcher, and Robert Rushton. Mr. Davies and Mr. Hobhouse, it will be understood, remained ashore.]

When at a distance, we waved our hands and hats, bidding adieu. The wind was completely in our teeth, but we made the passage in sixteen hours. The coast of Dover is very striking, though miserably barren-looking. The cliff is steep, though not such as Shakespear paints. The castle—at a distance, which is the only way I viewed it—is miserable. Sailing from England, I for a long time kept my eye upon its stern white cliffs, thinking on her who bade me join her remembrance with the last sight of my native soil.

[This points pretty clearly to a love-passage, perhaps a matrimonial engagement. As a fact Polidori never married. The lady may possibly have been Eliza Arrow, a relative in India, with whom he, at a rather earlier date, had interchanged various letters.]

They at last faded from my sight, and all on board looked dreary; the sea dashed over us, and all wore an aspect of grief. Towards night a most beautiful spectacle was seen by myself, who alone remained on deck. The stars shedding merely a twilight enabled me to see the phosphoric light of the broken foam in all its splendour. But the most beautiful moment was that of its first appearance: no sound around save the sullen rushing of the vessel, and the hoarse cries of the heaving sailor; no light save a melancholy twilight, which soothed the mind into forgetfulness of its grief for a while—a beautiful streak following the lead through the waves. We arrived at Ostend at 2 o'clock in the morning.

[Polidori's chronology is a little confusing here. If the party left Dover at 9 p.m. on April 25, and took sixteen hours in the sea-passage, they must have reached Ostend at 1 in the *afternoon*. There is also a confusion immediately afterwards, for he repeats the date for which he has already accounted, viz.]

April 26.—We passed through the gates, paying a franc a head, and went to the Cour Impériale. We were astonished at the excellent inn and good treatment, except that I got a dreadful headache from the smell of paint in my bedroom, and that the tea was perfumed.

[It was, I believe, at this point of the narrative that my aunt Charlotte Polidori cut out a peccant passage. I seem to remember the precise diction of it, which was this: "As soon as he reached his room, Lord Byron fell like a thunderbolt upon the chambermaid." Such at any rate was the substance of the statement. The other statement which my aunt excluded came somewhat further on, when Dr. Polidori was staying near Geneva. He gave some account of a visit of his to some haunt of the local Venus Pandemos. I think the police took some notice of it. The performance was not decorous, but was related without any verbal impropriety.]

Arising in the morning, I went upon a stroll round the town. Saw little girls of all ages with head-dresses; books in every bookseller's window of the most obscene nature; women with wooden shoes; men of low rank basking in the sun as if that would evaporate their idleness. The houses generally good old style, very like a Scotch town, only not quite so filthy. Very polite custom-house officers, and very civil waiters. Fine room painted as a panorama, all French-attitudinized. Went into a shop where no one spoke French. Tried German; half-a-dozen women burst out laughing at me. Luckily for myself, in a good humour; laughed with them. Obliged to buy two books I did not want, because I let a quarto fall upon a fine girl's head while looking at her eyes. Coaches of the most horrid construction; apparently some fine horses, others small. Fortifications look miserable. Once stood a fine siege, when 40,000 on one side and 80 on the other fed fowls and manured the fields. What for? For religion? No—for money. *There* was the spring of all. As long as only religion and rights were affected, bigoted religionists and wild republicans were alone concerned; but a step too far, and all was ruined.

[The allusion here is to the great siege of Ostend, 1601 to 1604.]

We set off at 3, with four horses. Postillion with boots to his hips, nankeens, leather hat with quaker brim, only neatly rounded with black riband; a blue and red coat, joined to which a most rascally face, with lips that went a few lines beyond the brim of his hat. A dreadful smacker of his whip, and a driver of four horses from the back of one of the hindermost. We were obliged to hire a calèche to send with our luggage. The rascal made us pay three times too much at each of his barriers; but, after having (on account of the horses not being ready at the next post) gone beyond his beat, he allowed the toll-keepers to be honest, and only take a few centimes instead of a franc. The country very flat, highly cultivated; sand, no waste. Roads paved in the middle, with trees on each side. Country, from the interspersion of houses, spires, cottages, etc., delightful; everything comfortable, no appearance of discontent.

We got out of our carriage at a place where the horses ate bread and hay, and walked on to a church-yard, where we found no tombstones, no funeral-pomp, no flattering eulogy, but simply a wooden cross at each grave's head and foot. On the side of the church-steeple, at a little height, was made a niche wherein statues formed a crucifixion, as an object to excite reverence and adoration of God in every passenger. We passed on, and arrived at Bruges at the fall of the evening. Our passports were dispensed with on our mentioning that we were not stopping. We entered one of the most beautiful towns I ever saw; every house seemed substantial—had some ornament either of fretwork or lines—all seem clean and neat. We stopped at the post. We were shown into the postmaster's parlour on our asking for something to eat— well furnished—better even than a common middleman's house in London. N.B.—Everywhere 6 francs for a bottle of Rhenish. Women generally pretty. Flemish face has no divinity—all pleasing more than beautiful—a sparkling eye in a full round. Their pictures of every age have the mark of their country.

As we went from Bruges, twilight softened all the beauty, and I do not know how to describe the feeling of pleasure we felt in going through its long roof-fretted streets, bursting on to spots where people were promenading amidst short avenues of trees. We passed on. At the gates I saw a boy with sand in his hand let it through his fingers laughingly, heedless of the myriads whose life hung upon each sand. We passed on at 10. We came to a village where we heard the sound of music. The innkeeper, on our enquiring what it was, asked us politely in to hear a concert of amateurs. We descended, and were gratified and surprised at hearing, in a village of 5000 souls, a full band playing difficult though beautiful music. One march particularly struck us. But what was our surprise, when the door opened, to view the group: none apparently above the rank of labourers, yet they met three times a week. In our country the amusement is to reel drunk as many. There was one figure manifestly consumptive, yet he was blowing an enormous trombone.

Within a few miles of Gand, I was wakened from a pleasant fireside in England by my companion saying "They have lost their way"; and, seeing a house near me, I jumped out to enquire, when to my great fear I saw it was deserted. I immediately suspected something, and went back for a pistol, and then thundered at the door; no one came. Looking round, I saw other houses; towards which upon my moving the postillion got off, and, telling me in French, as a consolation, that he could not understand it, went with me towards a house where there was light, and suddenly ran off. I immediately went to the carriage, and we gave sabres to the servants; when he ran back from out of sight, and knocked again at the door and roused two, who told us the way. By the by, we had crossed several times the bridge, and from the road and back again, whereas we had nothing to do but to go straight on, instead of which he crossed over and was going back in the direction of Bruges, when our servant stopped him. I cannot explain his conduct; he was dreadfully frightened.

We arrived at Ghent at 3 in the morning, and knocked some time at the gates, but at last, by means of a few francs, got through—passports not asked for. Got to the Hôtel des Pays Bas, where Count Artois resided while at Ghent. We were ushered into a splendid room, got excellent Rhenish, butter, cheese, etc., and went to bed.

April 27.—At Gand Charles the Ist of Spain was born. It was here he really showed the insufficiency of ambition and all the joys of manhood. After having at Brussels resigned to Philip his extensive dominions, he came here, and enjoyed many days while passing over the scenes of his youth, which neither the splendour attached to a European or an Indian crown nor to the conquests of his powerful and noble views could efface. He did not seek Pavia; no, it was at Gand that he sought for his last draught of worldly joy. The town was worthy of it, if beauty and antiquity, if riches and liberty with all their train, could render it worthy of him. This town has all the beauty of Bruges, but more extensive: finer houses perhaps, fine cathedral, fine paintings, fine streets, fine canal. The streets are perhaps the finest I have seen; not so unpleasantly regular as London, not so high, but more rich in outside.

We visited the Cathedral; and, after having been accustomed to the tinselly ornaments of our Catholic chapels, and the complete want of any in the Scotch and English churches, we were much pleased with the Cathedral's inside dress: paintings that were by the hand of masters; the fortune of a bishop expended in building the part near the altar in marble and statues not contemptible, united with the airy, high fretted roof and little light, impressive of awe. Under this Cathedral is the first Belgian church that was built in the reign of Charlemagne, 800 years, I think, after Christ. It is low-roofed, but so strong it bears the weight of the Cathedral upon it. There were several paintings preserved in it (before the date of oil-painting), where the colours are mixed with white of egg. Some curious tombs, where the different styles are evident. In the earliest tomb some of the draperies on the relief are in a bold fine style. One of the earliest has a bishop, where all his robes are carved out, with almost the threads of his vest. Others, however, are for general effect. We mounted 450 steps to the top of the steeple; whence we saw a complete horizon of plain, canals, intersecting trees, and houses and steeples thrown here and there, with Gand below at our feet. The sea at a distance, bound by the hands of man, which pointed "So far shall ye go and no farther." Bruges held in the horizon its steeples to our view, and many hamlets raised from out their surrounding wood their single spires to sight.

Treading again the iron-plated 450 stairs, we came into the street; and, mounting into a fiacre, we went to the Ecole de Dessin, where we found a well-provided gallery of paintings, with two students, unmoved by the visitors around, painting with the patience if not the genius of Dutch masters. They were rather a nuisance on the present occasion, as one covered with his machine a *chef d'œuvre* of Rubens, the *St. Roch amongst the Sick of the Plague.* There were two more by the same, of St. Roch and his Dog, etc. They were in a different style of colouring—sombre and grey; none of his gay draperies that I, no connoisseur, thought were constituents of Rubens. I saw—I do not remember whose, but—a picture that struck me much, *The Beheading of St. Jean,* where all the interest and beauty consisted in a dog smelling the dead body. There were two of Van Eyck, the first (according to the Flemish) who invented painting in oil; where the colouring was splendid and very like the stiffness of glass, but the faces were very good. Kruger had many here in honour of Charles the Vth. Amongst the others, one rather (though probably not meant as such) satirical: Charles, landing, takes hold of Dame Africa, who quietly points to a lion at her feet. Query—to drive him away? There was a *Judgment of Solomon* by the same, where the child was painted dead with most perfect nature; so much so that my companion, who is a father, could not bear its sight. Teniers has here a *Temptation of St. Anthony*: strange caricature—what a satire! If mere deceit is the acme of perfection, some Dutchmen may snatch the palm from either Apelles or Parrhasius. They paint boards with an engraving upon them, or a door,[1] or aught else, so inimitably that it deceived my friend. We went into the Academy of Casts, of Design, etc. There are generally 400 pupils in this town: many fall off annually without great advancement, and are trod on the heels by others.

We thence proceeded to another (we might say) cathedral. The steeple is not yet finished: the model is exhibited, with the curses of the Flemish exhibitors upon the "grande nation" for having taken the funds for its finishing. There are more good pictures than even in the Cathedral: the columns also please me more, being round, with a Gothic approach to Corinthian capital. The most beautiful painting I have yet seen is here (though I probably shall not be held out in my opinion by connoisseurs)— by Pollent, representing the trial of the true Cross upon a sick lady. The harmony of colouring, the soberness (without the commonly accompanying dulness) of the colouring, the good design and grouping, are, in my opinion, beautiful. Not even the splendid colouring of Rubens can make his pictures, in my eyes, equal to it.

[I do not know who is the painter termed Pollent by Polidori: on p. 50 there is the name Polenck, which may designate the same painter. Neither of these names can be traced by me in a catalogue of pictures in the Museum of Antwerp.]

There is one standing by it, of Vandyck, which has some sublimity in it, perhaps arising from indistinctness. It represents the effect of Christ's last sigh. By this altar stood twelve small pictures, hung out at this time for people to tread the "way of Calvary," representing the different stages of our Saviour's sufferings. There were many more pictures, but I cannot remember; seeing so many crowded in the Gallery put others out of my head. But there were painted in the Cathedral of St. Bavon, on the marble in the style of reliefs, different subjects of Scripture in a most masterly style; and so well were the shades managed that we could hardly believe the cicerone when he assured us they were paintings.

In the Gallery of Casts there were the statues of two English ladies of London by an artist who resided thirty years there, and upon his return bestowed these as his finest works. The faces, though not perfect or Grecian, I must say for my countrywomen, pleased me almost as much as any Venus de' Medici.

I have found the people polite, so far as showing the way and then not waiting for a reward—taking off their hats as if *you* had done them the favour.

April 28.—We set off at 8 this morning to go to Anvers; but, after having proceeded some way, one of the wheels refused to turn, and, after at the next village hammering a long while, I rode off in a passing calèche to Ghent, where I put a maréchal with his assistant into a voiture, and, mounting myself on horseback, returned to the coach. My horse was particularly fond of the shade; and, a house being near one of the barriers, he kindly stopped there to cool me. I, after waiting some time, began to press him to go forward, when he kicked etc. We went, while the carriage was being repaired, into a cottage, where all was extremely neat, and we saw two pictures in it that certainly would not shame the collection of many of our *soi-disant* cognoscenti. The old man was sick of a fever; and, upon giving him medicine, his kind half sympathetically fell ill of a toothache. Never did I see such chips of the old block as his two daughters. They were very kind. It being Sunday, we saw all the women of the village—all ugly: indeed, I have not seen a pretty woman since I left Ostend.

[This reference to April 28 as being a Sunday puts a stop to any preceding question as to the right day of the month, for in fact April 28, 1816, *was* a Sunday.]

On proceeding on our journey, we were stopped for our passports, and the fellow began bullying us, thinking we were French; but, when he heard we were English, he became cap in hand, and let us go: indeed, we have not yet shown our passports.

Having eaten, I issued forth in search of the Promenade, and found the canal with walks called La Copeure. Many ladies, all ugly without exception—the only pretty woman being fat and sixty. It very much resembled the Green Basin, where our West-end cits trot on one another's heels with all possible care: not quite so crowded. Coming back, I tourized to the Roi d'Espagne, where, as in a coffeehouse, I found a room full of disreputable women and card-tables. This, instead of the streets, is the lounge for such women. I went to the Café Grand, where by means of mirrors some excellent effects are produced. There also were billiards, cards, dice, etc. A cup of coffee, some centimes; a glass of lemonade, two sous: a woman presides at the end of the room.

"Lord Byron" was in the *Ghent Gazette*. Lord Byron encouraged me to write *Cajetan*, and to continue being a tragedian. Murray offered £150 for two plays, and £500 for my tour.

April 29.—Looking from my window, I saw a native dashing about in a barouche and four. There is in the town a society of nobles, and another of literati. Mr. Scamp has a fine collection of pictures, which I did not see. In Ghent, as well as in all other places where I have been, the barber's sign is Mambrino's helm. On the Sunday mornings there is a market for flowers in pot in the Place des Armes.

We set off at 11 in the morning, and passed through some fine villages: one of which, St. Nicholas, the mistress of the inn told me Buonaparte made into a town—"mais il n'y a pas des postes." The country is tiresomely beautiful. Fine avenues, which make us yawn with admiration; not a single variation; no rising ground—yes, one spot raised for a windmill. The landscape is as unchangeable as the Flemish face. The houses white-washed, with a row of trees before them; the roofs tiled, and the windows large. Indeed, the appearance of comfort in the places we have passed through is much greater than any I have seen in England. We have only seen one country-villa, and that very English: its pasture had the only firs we have yet seen. The avenues are sometimes terminated by a church or a house—the church very ugly; and both very tiresome, as they always prove much farther off than is at first expected. The ground cultivated, and without a weed—no waste ground. The plough moves as if cutting water, the soil is so light a sand. Women work in the fields as well as men. No more difference is found in the face of the inhabitants than in the face of the country. Nothing striking, all evenness, no genius, much stupidity. They seemed to spend all their fund of cleanliness upon their fields and houses, for they carry none about them.

An oldish man wears a three-cornered cocked hat, capacious breeches, black or blue stockings, buckles, and a great-coat; young, fancy travelling-caps. The women wear enormous gold earrings, large wooden shoes. Their dress is a kind of bed-gown, like the Scotch. Young girls of eight in town have their hair dressed with a net or cap. In towns and villages the better peasant-women wear a black silk mantle with a hood, that looks well. Multitudes of children everywhere, who tumble and run by the side of the carriage to gain a few centimes. In the larger villages the market-places are splendidly large, with a little square place in the middle, with pollards and a statue. The houses seem comfortable everywhere. Going into the house of a postmaster, we saw some English prints. At another, our servants having got down and comfortably seated themselves to a bottle of wine etc., the postmistress, on our getting out, took *us* for the servants, and told us "the messieurs Anglais were in yon room"—and then made us a thousand apologies. At every posthorse place there is kept a book of the posts: many barriers—every 1-1/2 mile.

At Gand they had told us we could not reach Anvers without passing the Scheldt at 2 o'clock—we passed it at 6-1/2.

The town of Antwerp makes a good figure at a distance, chiefly on account of its Cathedral, which has a very airy appearance, the steeple showing the sky between its meeting arches. About five steeples. The fortifications, which enabled Carnot to make such a defence, produce no great effect on the sight.

[The defence by Carnot was, when Polidori wrote, a quite recent event, 1814.]

The Scheldt is a fine river, not so large as our Thames, and covered with ugly Dutch vessels. We passed our coach in a boat.

[This coach was a formidable affair. According to Mr. Pryse Lockhart Gordon, it was "copied from the celebrated one of Napoleon taken at Genappe, with additions. Besides a *lit de repos*, it contained a library, a plate-chest, and every apparatus for dining."]

On landing, twenty porters ran off with our things to a cart. As they were passing, one in all the pomp of office stopped us, and asked for our passports, which (on handing to him) he detained, giving his directions to the police.

The older parts of Antwerp have a novel and strange effect by the gable-ends being all to the street, ornamented—very acute angles. The Place de Meer is fine. The old street, the finest I ever saw, has some fine houses. Many of the houses have English labels on them. In our sitting-room are two beds. Indeed, the towns are beautiful: their long streets, their houses all clean-stuccoed or white-washed, with strange old-fashioned fronts, the frequent canals, the large places and venerable cathedrals. Their places are much finer than our squares, for they contain trees, and are open without railing.

Went to the café, and saw all playing at dominoes. Read *The Times* till the 23rd. Fine furniture, everywhere of cherry-tree.

At Gand in the Cathedral the cicerone laid great stress on the choir-seats being all made of solid acajou. The master of the inn at Ghent assures me the carriage of Buonaparte was made in Paris—the body-carriage at Brussels: no English work. Plenty of Americans in the town.

April 30.—Got up late, and went to look at the carriage, and found that the back had been not of the best-made. Called a maréchal, who assured me it could not be better. Breakfasted. Then looked at an old calèche, for which asked 60 naps. Refused it.

Got, with a guide, a calèche to see the lions. The town is large: apparently, not a proportionable quantity of misery. Women better-looking. At all the fountains, Madonnas—and upon all the corners of the streets, with lamps before them. Lamps with reverberators strung on ropes into the middle of the streets. Went to the Cathedral. Everywhere we have been, dreadful complaints of French vandalism. In this chapel it has been shameless: once crowded with altars of marble, now there are about five—only two marble, the others painted in imitation. Pictures were stolen—altars sold by auction—only one saved, bought by a barber for a louis. The others, with all the tombs, monuments, everything, broken by these encouragers of the fine arts. So great was the ruin that there were five feet of fragments over the church—even the columns that support the roof were so much defaced that they were obliged, in restoring it, to pare them all much thinner. Some pictures were carried to Paris, of which some are now about to be replaced. It was the feast of St. Anthony, and many candles were burning about, and some relics were fixed above the doors. In many parts of the chapel were frames containing silver representations, very small, of bad limbs etc., offered by the devout. Many images over altars, dressed out in silk and taffeta: most common one, the Virgin Mary. Though the French acted with all the spirit of Vandals and true Gauls, yet to their very mischief is owing the greatest beauty of the Cathedral, the choir not being divided from the church, so that from one end to the other there is a complete perspective and one of the finest effects I have seen, the airiness and length being now proportionate. There is one great defect in the internal decorations—that they are Greek. What bad taste it is to ornament Gothic with Corinthian columns must be evident: to make it also more glaring, the marble is all coloured. There is here a fine marble altar-railing. Indeed, in all the churches we have here seen they are beautiful—especially where boys, called in Italian "puttini," are sculptured. The confessionals are of wood, with evangelical figures, nearly as large as life, between each box—not badly carved.

We went to see another church, wherein is the tomb of Rubens. [This is the Church of St. Jâques.]

It is in a chapel by itself, where annually a mass is said for his soul. It is worthy of him: ornamented by a painting, by himself, of St. George, and a statue he brought with him from Rome of the Holy Virgin. The church in which he is buried was saved from pillage by the priests belonging to it revolutionizing. It is crowded with altars and pictures—some Rubens, some Polenck, and others. There is a painting by Metsys, who originally was a maréchal, and who with his mere hammer formed the decorations to a pump, which are not bad. The Latin inscription on his monumental stone refers to a story related of him: that, upon courting the daughter of Francis Floris, the artist with indignation talked about the dirty rascal's impudence, he being merely a blacksmith; on which Metsys set off for Rome, and upon his return asked the daughter to introduce him to her father's room of painting: where, finding a picture not finished, he painted a bee—that excited the indignation of Floris's pocket-handkerchief, and gained him his daughter. I have seen the picture, and it might be true. The pump is not bad, being merely beaten into shape. On the top is a giant who used to cut off merchants' gains by means of tolls, andtheir hands by means of axes. He used to throw an iron band into the scales of his tradesmen; and from thence, 'tis said, Antwerp got its name.

[This may be "said": but a less legendary derivation of the

41

Flemish name Antwerpen is "aent werf," or "on the wharf."]

The sides of this church all along are lined with confessionals.

In the Church des Augustins we saw Rubens's *Assembly of the Saints*, from Paris; where he has shown how weak he could be in composition, and in vanity—for it is the third picture in which he has put himself in St. George's armour. The composition is confused, without an object to fix the attention. A Vandyck near him is much superior.

[Polidori's observations about Flemish paintings are generally indicative of liking, more or less: but Byron went dead against them. In a letter of his to his half-sister, Mrs. Leigh, written from Brussels on May 1, 1816, we find: "As for churches and pictures, I have stared at them till my brains are like a guide-book: the last (though it is heresy to say so) don't please me at all. I think Rubens a very great dauber, and prefer Vandyck a hundred times over—but then I know nothing about the matter. Rubens's women have all red gowns and red shoulders; to say nothing of necks, of which they are more liberal than charming. It may all be very fine, and I suppose it may be art, for 'tis not nature." Again, in a letter to John Murray from Milan, October 15, 1816: "The Flemish school, such as I saw it in Flanders, I utterly detested, despised, and abhorred."]

Here is also the famous picture of Jordaens, of *The Martyrdom of St. Apollonia*. Colouring approaches Rubens; but abominable composition—crowded, large, numerous figures in a small space. There were some modern paintings of existing artists—meagre statue-compositions.

In the Musée we saw many Rubenses. The famous *Descent from the Cross*: the effect of the white sheet is wonderfully beautiful. Picture's drawing I do not like. The Christ seems not dead, as there is certainly action; but the colouring is splendidly rich. The *Crucifixion* near it, inferior in all. In a sketch near it he has not succeeded so well in the white sheet, it being not so splendidly white. We could only see the side-pieces of the great *Crucifixion*, as the large piece was being framed. In these there is much caricature drawing: a woman rising from the dead—surely a woman large as Guy Warwick giant's wife, if ever he had one: caricature physiognomies, and most hellish egregious breasts, which a child refuses, with horror in its face. His horses have much spirit—true Flemish size. Indeed, divest Rubens of his rich apparel, and he is a mere dauber in design. There is a *Mary going to Elizabeth*, looking more like a cardinal: indeed, my companion, Lord Byron, took her for one of the red-vested nobles. No divinity about his Christs; putrefaction upon his Gods; exaggerated passion about his men and women, painted not all-concealing. In his picture of *The Adoration of the Magi*, query did he not intend to play upon the people by passing off a caricature for a religious painting? The royal personage in green seems as if his eyes had grown big after dinner. He has no costume properly applied: the Virgin in the manger is dressed meretriciously in silks and lace. Then look at our blessed Saviour showing His wounds. His finest painting is his *Crucifixion* in which is the white sheet: but there are defects. What then must be the power of colouring which causes you to view his paintings with pleasure! It is like melodious music which makes you forget the absurd words of an old English song.

Vandyck, in my opinion, was much superior to Rubens. His colouring, near his, is sombre; but then his design is more perfect, his impressions remain longer in the mind distinct, and do not fade away into ideas of red and blue round white. A little *Crucifix* of his is worth his rival's largest paintings. His *Christ Dead* is beautiful, wherein are contained the Blessed Virgin, St. Mary Magdalene, and St. John weeping: the different expressions of grief, the unison of colouring with the subject, the composition, all excellent.

From the Cathedral we went to see the works of Napoleon. We first saw the Basins. They are not so large as our West India Docks—square—but are capable of holding ships of the line; there are two. Between them is what was formerly the Hanseatic Hall, now magazines. When the English were last here they threw bombs, but this was of no avail; dung was put upon the ships, and men were at hand in case of fire. From the Basins we went along the quays—very long, along the labouring Scheldt; then into the places for marine arsenals, where the vessels were on the stocks—the finest works I ever saw, now useless through our jealousy. The rope-house, quite finished, is enormously long, and is to be pulled down. The timbers for the ship were numbered, and carried to Amsterdam. The citadel was mean-looking, though so strong. The chief batteries are as old as Alva's time—there was one pointed out as erected by Colonel Crawford. Before Napoleon's time there was little done towards the formation of these basins and others; but, said our guide, "he decreed they should be made, and they appeared." They are all surrounded with high walls to hinder the escape of the employed. Carnot has commanded here twice. He was rather disliked, yet they had rather have him than any other. They all agree in his genius. In the time of the Walcheren business the English were expected with open arms: only three hundred soldiers—Bernadotte was general. The siege was not very strict on the last occasion, and no mischief was done on either side. In the Basins there have been twenty-six line. In the dread of a siege all the suburbs were destroyed and all the trees around. The suburbs rose immediately, the trees in years. In the citadel there are 1500 forçats. Sometimes the number exceeds 2000.

Having seen thus much, we returned, lunched, and rode off. Hardly gone a little way when our carriage broke down. The trees are more various—vegetation more advanced—more inequality of ground—more pollards—more apparent misery—more villas, some pretty—more clipped hedges—more like England—fine, large, town-like villages. Carriage broke again—walked to Malines—arrived there at ten. Women improve.

At Antwerp, in one church on the outside, saw a supposed exact imitation of the Sepulchre, though I do not know how it came seated "in purgatory"; as there certainly is a place so called round it, full ofthe damned and flames. The place is grotto-

work. Within there is a representation of our Lord swathed in
linen. All over there are statues, so so. David is at a respectable
distance from purgatory: this makes it the more remarkable that
the Sepulchre is seated in purgatory. Indeed, indeed, there is
much absurdity.

There is an academy for drawing and painting, with a museum.
The Place is in a garden.

On arriving at Malines we found Mr. Pradt gone from his
bishopric amongst his brethren; and we are assured he was a
"vraiment français," and that he was not a "Catholique," and that
this town wanted a "vraiment Catholique."

[The Abbé de Pradt, born in Auvergne in 1759, had been a
champion of the monarchy in the Constituent Assembly of 1789-
91. Napoleon made him Archbishop of Malines towards 1809,
but afterwards viewed him with disfavour. He resigned the
Archbishopric in 1816, receiving a pension. He wrote a number
of books on political and public matters, and died in 1837.]

The country from Antwerp to Malines becomes more and
more like England: trees more various, not the same dead
flat but varied with gentle swells, many pollards, and more
miserable cottages.

There is in the Cathedral [in Antwerp] a painting by
Floris—the one on which is the bee—where he has shown great
imagination and fire in the devils. It is the victory of the angels
when fighting against the devils.

May 1.—As soon as up, I went to the Cathedral, which has
a fine tower. On entering I saw many pictures. None that I saw
seemed particularly good. The church was pretty full of people,
who really seemed devout. They were not the old and weak, but
there was of every age. The young maiden was seen by the side of
decrepit age, beauty by deformity, childhood by manhood. The
effect on the mind is contagious. Many masses were going on at
the same time. A woman went round for money for the chairs.
Here I saw the first Christian caryatides.

We soon set off for Brussels. Between V. and that town the road is beautiful; a canal on one side, fine trees forming a long avenue diversified with glimpses of a rich country. We passed the Castle of Lac, the former residence of Buonaparte. It has a fine front upon an eminence, but the dome stands forth in glaring ugliness. We entered Brussels by the Allée Verte, a fine promenade.

Brussels, the old town, is not so fine as Antwerp, Ghent, or Bruges. The Grand Marché is very beautiful, only the buildings seem to be neglected. Fine public offices, with a tall spire, on one side—the Mairie opposite. The Place Royale is very fine; the fronts of the houses and hotels around seeming together to form parts of one great palace; and the church on one side, with the housy wings, has a fine effect in spite of the ugly tower at the top. The gardens are beautiful with green, and well laid out in walks, with groups and termites—the Palace opposite. The entrance from the Place Royale presents a fine front, and the suburbs round it are also good. We are at the Hôtel d'Angleterre. Saw *Morning Chronicles*, which are again dutysied.

Brussels was not at all fortified in the Waterloo time. The Germans at one time had retreated as far as the gates, which were obliged to be shut against them. In case of a retreat there would have been a pleasant rush, almost as great as at a fashionable rout, as they must all have passed through Brussels. The carriage was put under hand. Crowds of English.

May 2.—We have seen many, many soldiers. No wonder they were light of foot when not more heavy of age, for none have beards yet except some few cavalry.

The English women are the only good-looking women in Brussels; though, with true English Bullism, they vest *here* a complete Anglomanian costume, preserving their French fashions for the English winds to waft. The women of Brabant and the Netherlands are all ugly to the eye after the piquant begins to pall, for there are no regular beauties or beauty of expression, except that levity which tells of lightness of cares and youth.

It is not for a foreigner to call a thing absurd because it does not tally with his ideas, or the ladies' costume, except the black mantle, should be put down as such by me. The men also are short and bad-looking, either consummate impudence or complete insignificance—no individuality. The indelicacy of these Belgians is gross; all kinds of disgusting books publicly sold, and exposed to the eyes of all young damsels—beastliness publicly exhibited on the public monuments—fountains with men vomiting with effort a stream of water—and still worse. The town (Brussels) is situated on an eminence, and is really poor in comparison of the other Belgic towns by us seen.

After dinner, having dressed, I went, having written two letters, to the theatre. Mounting a voiture, I was soon there. Ascending some stairs, I came to a door where, after some knocking, a man took my money, and gave me tickets, which, changed twice, brought me to the first row of boxes. The first look at the lobbies was sufficient to give me an idea of all the rest—misery, misery, misery, wherever one turned—to the floor, to the ceiling, to the wall, to the box-wall, all garret of the St. Giles style. Most of the doors had *Abonnement* written on them. I got into one, and what a sight! boxes dirty with filth. One chandelier was sufficient for the pockets of a Brussels manager, hung from the middle. Pit divided into two parts of different prices, boxes into three, and a gallery. Chairs, not benches, in the boxes. Ladies came and sat and talked, and talked and sat and stood, and went away. Many English ladies. Orchestra began—all violins, seven in all. Curtain up—a farce: no—it did not make me laugh. How call that a theatrical amusement which only seems fitted to excite the pleasurable sensation of yawning? It was French. An actress, the best amongst them, spoke French like a base pig; another contorted the fine lady into one with a paralytic stroke after sitting up at cards; the gentlemen like purlieu-bullies; and high life was copied from the waiting-maids of butchers' ladies. I was a little surprised at the applause that a lady actress gained. It moved me astonishingly: not her acting, but the lookers-on acting pleasure. At last came the wind whistling through the reeds, the thunder-hurling cheeks, and lashing hands, to my great admiration. It moved phlegm.

One who was to act Blondel was vomiting at home. I went behind the scenes, and saw dismay in every face, and terror in every limb. The curtain drew up, and the play began. Hisses, hisses, hisses. It fell, and fear increased. Some time was spent in cogitation. The venturous gold-decked hero advanced, retired, was rebuked by the police and forced to advance. Hisses. He said to the audience he was forced to advance. They listened, and quiproquos commenced between the players and the audience, with the sonorous hiss of anger. The police saw all was in vain, and ordered the actors off the boards. I in the meantime was chatting with two apparent goddesses, who very concisely explained the trembling of the actors, etc., by telling me of real showers of eggs, etc. As I left the house I heard groans and hollow sounds, and cries of "Give me back my money: I am an *abonné*, and have seen nothing." I ran—I and the police pushing on, the mob pushing us back, etc. Going along the lobbies, what was my wonder to stumble on a bookseller's shop, where was an assemblage of delicacies fit for the modest, and wondrous delicate!

May 3.—I saw in the street three dogs, of the bulldog race, dragging up a hill at a good pace what I am sure two men would not have strength to drag. I saw also a goat fastened to a child's car. I went all over the town for a calèche—bought one for 75 louis. In the evening, having procured redingotes (which I did not use), we mounted a coach and drove to ——. Returned home, ate, and slept.

May 4.—Having risen, foolishly paid 40 naps. to the coachmaker. My Lord and servant stepped into the calèche. I and a servant got on horseback, and went to Waterloo. We soon entered Soignies, which on both sides formed a beautiful wood (not forest, for it was not wild on either side) for several miles. The avenue it formed varied in length: sometimes the end was formed by a turn of the road, sometimes by the mere perspective effect of narrowing. The trees are all young—none of above thirty years' growth. We then reached Waterloo, where were the head-quarters of Napoleon. An officious host pressed us to order dinner. We ran from his pressing, and advancing came to St. Jean, where the boys continued the offerings we first had at Waterloo of buttons, books, etc. This was the village which gave the French name to the battle, I believe, as it was the spot which Napoleon tried to gain. The view of the plain, as we advanced to the right, struck us as fields formed almost with the hopes that spirit and war would make their havoc here. Gentle risings, sufficient to give advantage to the attacked—few hedges—few trees. There was no sign of desolation to attract the passer-by; if it were not for the importunity of boys, and the glitter of buttons in their hands, there would be no sign of war. The peasant whistled as blithely, the green of Nature was as deep, and the trees waved their branches as softly, as before the battle. The houses were repaired. Only a few spots with white plaster between the bricks pointed out the cannon's ruin; and in ruins there was only Hougoumont, which was attacked so bravely and defended so easily—at least so I should imagine from the few killed in the garden and the appearance of the whole, while so many French lay dead in the field. In the garden were only 25 English killed, while in the field 1500; and on the other side 600 French, not counting the wounded, were slain. Indeed, the gallantry, the resolution and courage, which the French displayed in attacking this place, guarded from the heights by our cannon, and by our soldiers through the loop-holes, would alone ennoble the cause in which they fought. Before arriving at Hougoumont, the spots where Hill, Picton, and the Scotch Greys did their several deeds, were pointed out to us. The spot which bore the dreadful charge of cavalry is only marked by a hedge. The cuirassiers advancing, the Scots divided—showed a masked battery, which fired grape into the adverse party's ranks—then it was the Scots attacked. I do not now so much wonder at their victory. The cuirasses which we saw were almost all marked with bullets, lance- and sabre-cuts. Buonaparte and the French, our guide said, much admired the good discipline and undaunted courage of the short-kilted Scot.

Going forward, the spot at which the Prussians, the lucky gainers of the battle, emerged, was pointed out to us—and, a little farther on, we were shown the spot where Colonel Howard, my friend's cousin, was buried before being carried to England. Three trees, of which one is cut down, mark the spot, now ploughed over. At Hougoumont we saw the untouched chapel where our wounded lay, and where the fire consumed the toes of a crucifix. We there inscribed our names amongst cits and lords. We found here a gardener who pointed out the garden—the gate where the French were all burnt—the gap in the hedge where the French attempted, after the loss of 1500 men, to storm the place—the field, quarter of an acre, in which were heaps of Gallic corpses. The gardener and the dog, which we saw, had been detained at Hougoumont by General Maitland in case of a retreat. The peasants declare that from 4 to 5 the affair was very, very doubtful, and that at the last charge of the Imperial Guards Napoleon was certain of being in Brussels in *quatre heures*. Wellington, after the defeat of the Prussians etc., on the 17th went to Waterloo, and determined where he would place each corps. This was a great advantage: but, in spite of the excellence of his position, he would certainly have been defeated had it not been for the fortunate advance of the Prussians. From Hougoumont we went to the red-tiled house which is the rebuilding of the house where was Buonaparte's last station and head-quarters. It was from this spot that he viewed the arrival of the Prussians, under the idea of their being the corps of Grouchy. It was here he felt first the certainty of defeat, just after he had led the old Imperial Guard, in the certainty of victory, to his last attack. La Belle Alliance next appeared along the road, here where Wellington and Blücher met. The name is derived from a marriage in the time of peace: it is now applicable to a war-meeting. Thence we returned to St. Jean, after going again to Hougoumont. There we were shown cuirasses, helms, buttons, swords, eagles, and regiment-books. We bought the helms, cuirasses, swords, etc., of an officer and soldier of cuirassiers, besides eagles, cockades, etc. Beggars, the result of

English profusion. A dinner, measured by some hungry John Bull's hungry stomach. We rode off the field, my companion singing a Turkish song—myself silent, full gallop cantering over the field, the finest one imaginable for a battle. The guide told us that the account Buonaparte's guide gave of him after the battle was that he only asked the road to Paris, not saying anything else.

At Hougoumont various spots were pointed out: amongst the rest the one where Maitland stood watching a telegraph on the neighbouring rise, which told him what was going on on both sides.

We rode home together through Soignies forest—black. The twilight made the whole length of the road more pleasing. On reaching home, we found the coach was jogged; so much so that it would not allow us to put confidence in it, etc. At last we gave it into Mr. Gordon's hands. My friend has written twenty-six stanzas (?) to-day—some on Waterloo.

There are a few points in this narrative of May 4 which call for a little comment.

1. As to "the spot where Colonel Howard, my friend's cousin, was buried before being carried to England." Few passages in the 3rd canto of *Childe Harold*, which in its opening deals with Byron's experiences in these days, are better known than the stanzas (29 to 31) where he celebrates the death of "young gallant Howard." Stanza 30 is the one most germane to our immediate purpose—

> "There have been tears and breaking hearts for thee,
> And mine were nothing, had I such to give.
> But, when I stood beneath the fresh green tree
> Which living waves where thou didst cease to live,
> And saw around me the wide field revive
> With fruits and fertile promise, and the Spring
> Come forth her work of gladness to contrive,
> With all her reckless birds upon the wing,
> I turn'd from all she brought to those she could not bring."

2. The statement that "the coach was jogged" refers to that calèche which had been just bought in Brussels for the servants—not to the elaborate travelling-carriage. Some trouble ensued over the calèche. The coachmaker who had sold it tried to make Lord Byron pay up the balance of the price. Not carrying his point, he got a warrant-officer to seize a different vehicle, a chaise, belonging to the poet. The latter, so far as appears, took no further steps.

3. To write twenty-six stanzas in one day is no small feat; especially if these are the nine-line stanzas of *Childe Harold*, and if the substantial work of the day consisted in riding from Brussels to Waterloo and back, and deliberately inspecting the field of battle. The entry, as written by Charlotte Polidori, stands thus—"26 st.," which I apprehend can only mean "stanzas." If one were to suppose that the stanzas thus written on May 4 were the first twenty-six stanzas of *Childe Harold*, canto 3 (but this of course is not a necessary inference), Byron now got up to the stanza which begins

"And wild and high the 'Camerons' gathering' rose."

I made up my accounts, and was not a little startled by a deficit of 10 napoleons, which I at last found was a mere miscalculation. Rode about thirty miles in all.

Forgot to say I saw Sir Nath[aniel] Wraxall at Dover, who, having introduced himself to Lord Byron as a friend *de famille*, began talking, knocking his feet in rattattat, still all the while oppressed by feeling very awkward.

[I do not find in Byron's correspondence any reference to this interview, on April 25 or 26, with Sir Nathaniel Wraxall. But, in his letter of April 25 to his half-sister, he mentions that he met on the 24th with Colonel Wildman, an old school-fellow, and later on the purchaser of Newstead Abbey, who gave him some details concerning the death of Colonel Howard at Waterloo.]

At Brussels, the people were in a great stew, the night of the battle of Waterloo—their servants and others waking them every minute to tell them the French were at the gates. Some Germans went there with mighty great courage, in flight. Lord W[ellington?] sent to a colonel to enquire whether he was going to fly from or to the battle, giving him his choice to act in either way. On hearing this, the said colonel boldly faced about, and trotted to Brussels with his troop. A supernumerary aide-de-camp, the brother of N., with two others, was riding between the ranks while the French were firing; when, ours crying out "They aim at you," all three were struck in the jaw, much in the same place, dead. After the battle, a friend asking what was become of N., the serjeant pointed to his feet, saying "There," which was fact. Dacosta, the guide, says that Buonaparte was cool and collected till the Prussians arrived; that then he said to Bertrand, "That appears to be the Prussian eagle"; and, upon Bertrand's assenting, his face became momentarily pale. He says that, when he led up the Imperial Guard, on arriving at the red-tiled house, he went behind a hillock, so as not to be seen, and so gave them the slip. Wellington acted the soldier when he should have acted the general, and the light-limbed dancer when he should have been the soldier. I cannot, after viewing the ground, and bearing in mind the men's superior courage, give Wellington the palm of generalship that has been snatched for him by so many of his admirers. Napoleon only took one glass of wine from the beginning of the battle to the end of his flight.

May 5.—Got up at ten from fatigue. Whilst at breakfast, there came a Mr. Pryse Gordon for L[ord] B[yron]. I entertained him. He has been to Italy, and travelled a great deal—a good-natured gentleman. Took him to see the carriage: there he introduced me to his son by means of a trumpet. After his departure we set off for the Château du Lac, where we found the hind front much finer than the other for want of the startling (?) dome and low windows. It has all its master-apartments on the ground-floor: they are extremely well laid out both with regard to comfort and magnificence—they were furnished by Nap[oleon]. We saw the bed where Josephine, Marie Louise, and the Queen of Holland, have been treading fast on one another's heels. The hall for concerts divides the Emperor's from the Empress' rooms—it has a rich appearance, and is Corinthian. The flooring of the Emperor's is all wood of different colours—checked—having to my eye a more pleasing appearance than the carpeted ones of the Empress. I sat down on two chairs on which had sat he who ruled the world at one time. Some of his eagles were yet remaining on the chairs. The servant seemed a little astonished at our bowing before them.

We returned, it raining all the while. After dinner Mr. G[ordon] came for us to go to coffee. We went, and were graciously received; Lord B[yron] as himself, I as a tassel to the purse of merit. I there saw a painting of Rembrandt's wife or mother by himself, which was full of life, and some verses by Walter Scott written in the hostess' album, where he says Waterloo will last longer than Cressy and Agincourt. How different! They only agree in one thing—that they were both in the cause of injustice. The novels of Casti were presented to me by Mr. Gordon, which I was rather surprised at. We came over. Scott writes in M[rs]. G[ordon's] book—

"For one brief hour of deathless fame" [Scott].

"Oh Walter Scott, for shame, for shame" [Byron].

[The novels of the Abate Casti (who died in 1803) are notoriously licentious: hence, I suppose, Polidori's surprise at the presentation of them by Mr. Gordon. Byron, it is stated by this gentleman, was asked by Mrs. Gordon on May 5 to write some lines in her album. He took the volume away with him, and on the following day brought it back, having inserted in it the two opening stanzas on Waterloo forming part of canto 3 of *Childe Harold*—from

"Stop, for thy tread is on an empire's dust,"

to

"He wears the shattered links of the world's broken chain"]

May 6.—Mr. G[ordon] and son came while at breakfast; gave us letters, etc. Saw the little child again; B[yron] gave it a doll.

It may be excusable to suppose that this trifling incident is not wholly foreign to a stanza, 54, in the 3rd canto of *Childe Harold*. This stanza comes immediately after Byron has begun to speak of the Rhine, and incidentally of the affection which his half-sister bore him. Then he proceeds—

"And he had learn'd to love—I know not why,
For this in such as him seems strange of mood—
The helpless looks of blooming infancy,
Even in its earliest nurture. What subdued,
To change like this, a mind so far imbued
With scorn of man, it little boots to know:
But thus it was; and, though in solitude
Small power the nipp'd affections have to grow,
In him this glow'd when all beside had ceased to glow."

The *carrossier* came. Set off at two, passing through a country increasing in inequalities. We arrived first at Louvain, where we saw the outside of a beautiful Town-hall, which is one of the prettiest pieces of external fretwork I have seen. Thence we went to Tirlemont, where was a Jubilee. Saints and sinners under the red canopy (the sky dirty Indian-ink one) were alike in the streets. Every street had stuck in it, at a few paces from the house-walls, fir-branches 16 or 17 feet high, distant from one another 5 or 6 feet. Thence to St. Trond, where we ate—and slept, I suppose. The country is highly cultivated, and the trees older. The avenues have a more majestic appearance from the long swells of ground and the straight roads, but there is more squalid misery than I have seen anywhere. The houses are many of them mud, and the only clean part about them is the white-wash on the external walls. Dunghills before some must be trodden on before entering the houses. The towns also fall off greatly in neat and comfortable looks. The walls round them look ruined and desolate, and give a great idea of insecurity. We put the servants on board-wages.

May 7.—Set off from St. Trond at 11. The country is highly cultivated; continual hill and dale; lower orders miserable in perfection; houses built of mud, the upper storeys of which are only built of beams, the mud having fallen off. Bridges thrown over the dirt they were too idle to remove. Dunghills at their doors, and ditches with black fetid water before their first step. Liège has a pretty neighbourhood, but the town itself is filthy and disagreeable. They visited our passports here at three different places. The hill above the town is enormously steep; and from some way beyond it has a beautiful view of Liège with its towers and domes—of the country with its many cots and villas—and of the Meuse. The road now lies through a scene where cottages are spread like trees, and hedges like furrows of corn, the fields are so minutely divided. A little farther still we had a most splendid view through many miles. From a valley we could see everything clearly, crowded in a blue tint, and in a river through it we could see the shadows of the trees. The cottages are improving, and the roads becoming the worst ever seen; paved still, but so horridly hilled and vallied that the rolling of the carriage is like the rolling of a ship.

We came at last to Battice; but before entering we passed by a village where beggar little cherubs came to the carriage-side, and running cried out, "Donnez-nous quelque chose, Monsieur le chef de bataillon"; another, "Monsieur le général." And a third little urchin, who gesticulated as well as cried, perceiving the others had exhausted the army, cried, "Un sou, Messieurs les rois des Hanovériens!" We arrived at Battice, where beggars, beggars. There we found horses just come in.

After debate (wherein I was for Aix-la-Chapelle, L[ord] B[yron] for stopping) we set off; and such a jolting, rolling, knocking, and half-a-dozen etc., as our carriage went through, I never saw, which put L[ord] B[yron] to accusing me of bad advice; clearing however as the road mended. The rain fell into a pond, to be illuminated by sunshine before we reached Aix-la-Chapelle at half-past twelve.

May 8.—Got up late. Went to see the Cathedral: full of people, lower ranks, hearing mass. Miserable painting, architecture, etc. Saw also a church wherein was no particular picture or anything. At Liège the revolutionists had destroyed the fine Cathedral.

A German boy who led me about Aix-la-Chapelle, on my asking him in broken German about the baths, led me to a very different place. I was astonished to find myself in certain company. The baths are hot sulphuretted-hydrogen-impregnated water. The sulphur-beds are only shown to dukes and kings: so a kingdom is good for something. I saw the baths themselves: like others, not very clean-looking.

We left Aix-la-Chapelle at twelve, going through a fine country, with no hedges but fine woods in the distance. We arrived at St. Juliers, strongly fortified, where they took our names at entering and at exiting. It is a neat town, and was besieged last year. We were at the post taken by a man for Frenchmen, and he told us we had been driven from Russia by a band of the Emperor. He seemed to be very fond of them, and gave as a reason that he had been employed by them for many years. And, I forgetfully saying, "What! were they here?"—"Yes, and farther." I answered, "Jusqu'à Moscou." "Oui, et presque plus loin." That "presque" means much. The French were not generally liked, I believe. The lower orders perhaps liked them, but the middle, I doubt. But I cannot say; I may perhaps be influenced by the opinion of a beautiful face of this town, who, on my asking her whether the *dames n'aimaient pas beaucoup les Français*, answered, "*Oui, les dames publiques.*"

We find it a great inconvenience that the Poste is a separate concern, and generally pretty distant from the inn. The women are many of them very beautiful, and many of them, as well as the men, have fine dark eyes and hair. The men wear ear-rings, and curl their hair; which, if I remember rightly, was the custom in the time of Tacitus. Many of the women wear their hair combed quite back, and upon it a little square piece of linen. The French were particularly polite during the siege.

We entered the dominions of the King of Prussia a little beyond Battice. It causes a strange sensation to an Englishman to pass into one state from another without crossing any visible line. Indeed, we should not have perceived that we had, if we had not been stopped by a Belgian guard who asked us if we had anything to declare. The difference is, however, very striking. The men, the women, everything, improve—except the cottages. The people look cleaner, though everything else is dirty; contrary to the Belgians, they seem to collect their cleanliness upon themselves, instead of throwing it upon their cots, tins, trees, and shrubs.

We arrived at Cologne after much bad, sandy, heavy road, at 11. The pavement begins to be interrupted after Aix, but ends almost entirely after St. Juliers. Cologne is upon a flat on the Rhine. We were groaning at having no sight of far-famed Cologne, when we came suddenly under its battlements and towers. We passed through its fortifications without question. After having found the gates shut, and feed the porter, we found inns full, and at last got into the Hôtel de Prague.

May 9.—Got up very bad.[2] Sat down to breakfast. Just done, we heard some singing. Enquiry told us, buyable. Got them up. A harp played by a dark-haired German, pretty, and two fiddlers. She played and sang *The Troubadour*, which brought back a chain of Scotch recollections, and a German song; then a beautiful march, in which the music died away and then suddenly revived. After a waltz we dismissed them. We both mounted a voiture, and drove through the town to the Cathedral. Great part pulled down by the revolutionists, and the roof of the nave obliged to be restored with plain board—a staring monument over Gallic ruin. There is fine stained glass, and the effect of its being very high and variegated in the choir is beautiful. We saw a fine painting here by Kalf: vide *Taschbuch*. The tomb of the three kings said to be worth three millions of francs, and an immensely rich treasury wherein was a sacrament worth one million of francs. In falling down a step I broke a glass, for which they at first would not take anything—which at last cost me three francs. Kept countenance amazingly well.

Went to see St. Ursula's Church, where we were shown virgins' skulls of ninety years old, male and female, all jumbled into a mass of 11,000 virgins' bones arranged all in order—some gilt, etc. A whole room bedecked with them. All round, indeed, whatever we saw were relics, skulls; some in the heads of silver-faced busts, some arranged in little cells with velvet cases, wherein was worked the name of each. Paintings of St. Ursula, etc. Asked for a piece out of the masses: only got a smile, and a point of a finger to an interdiction in Latin, which I did not read.

We went to see a picture of Rubens, *The Nailing of St. Peter to a Cross*; the best design, though not very good, I yet have seen of his. A German artist copying it spoke English to us.

Returned home. Sent my name to Professor Wallraf: got admission. Found a venerable old man who has spent his life in making a collection of paintings and other objects of vertù belonging to his country, Cologne, which he intends leaving to his native town.

[This is no doubt the Wallraf who was joint founder of the celebrated Wallraf-Richartz Museum in Cologne. The statement which ensues as to an early oil-painter named Kaft is noticeable; whether correct I am unable to say. The Wallraf-Richartz Museum does not contain any painting by Tintoretto to which the name *Campavella* could apply: there is a fine picture by him of *Ovid and Corinna*.]

Many pictures were extremely good, especially painting of individuals. Kaft was a native of this town, who painted in oil before oil-painting was known. Saw some Poussins, Claude Lorraines. Some moderate. A Tintoretto of *Campavella* beautiful:

colouring and drawing strong and expressive. A Rembrandt and a Teniers, etc. A master of Rubens. A copy in colours from the drawing of Raphael by one of his disciples. Cologne has stamped more coins than some empires, and has coined twenty-six kinds of gold. He had made drawings of them, but the revolution stopped it. The revolutionary Gauls, he said with a tear in his eye, had destroyed many very valuable relics of Cologne; and, pointing to a leaf of a missal with another tear, he said: "Many like this once adorned our churches: this is all." He had the original manuscript of Albert le Grand, *History of Animals*; Titian's four designs of the Cæsars at Polenham, with his own handwriting; the Albert Durer's sketch of Christ's head which belonged to Charles II; and a painting of Albert Durer's Master. [3] He wishes for a copy of any of Caxton's printing in England.

Went to buy some books. Found Miss Helmhoft, a fine woman. Had a long confab. Bought more books than I wanted. Heard her spout German poetry that I did not understand; and laughed at the oddity of her gesticulation, which she took for laughter at the wit of a poet who was describing the want of a shirt—and was highly pleased.

The French destroyed convents, and made of them public places for walking.

Have been taken for servants, Frenchmen, merchants—never hardly for English. Saw the Rhine last night—fine mass of water, wide as the Thames some way below Blackwall; but no tide, and very deep. Town dirty, very decayed, badly paved, worse lighted, and few marks of splendour and comfort.

May 10.—We have seen crucifixes for these four days at every turn, some made of wood, some of stone, etc. Set off, after having defeated the imposition of a postman, to Bonn; the scenery not anything particular till we see the Seven Hills, a large amphitheatre on the right, glimpses on the left of the Rhine, and the Seven Hills. Bonn at last appeared, with its steeples, and on the neighbouring hills castles and cots, towers, and (not) towns.[4]

I saw yesterday a picture of Rembrandt's with three lights in it very well managed, at Wallraf's.

Saw R. Simmons' writing in the police-book at Bonn, and wrote to Soane.

[This was John, the son of Sir John Soane, founder of the Soane Museum in Lincoln's Inn Fields.]

The innkeeper makes you put your name—whence—whither—profession and age—every night. Rogues all of them, charging much.

May 11.—We saw the first vines a little before entering Cologne some days ago. We left Bonn at eleven, the town having nothing in particular. The Seven Hills were the first that struck our sight on one of the highest pinnacles in Drachenfels, now a mere ruin, formerly a castle of which many a tale is told. There was by the roadside a monument raised upon the spot where one noble brother killed another. Crucifixes all the way. We had the river on one side, whence rose hills (not mountains) cultivated halfway for vines—and the rest, nuts, shrubs, oak, etc. Towers on pinnacles, in ruin; villages (with each its spire) built of mud.

Cultivation in a high degree; no hedges, ground minutely divided into beds rather than fields; women working in the fields; ox and horse ploughing; oxen draw by their heads alone. Peasantry happy-looking and content. Two points particularly struck us—the Drachenfels, and the view at a distance before coming to Videnhar when the distant hills were black with the rain. But the whole way it is one of the finest scenes, I imagine, in the world. The large river with its massy swells and varied towered banks.

We changed horses at Bemagne, and passed over a road first cut by Aurelius, Theodoric, and Buonaparte. B[uonaparte]'s name is everywhere. Who did this? N[apoleon] B[uonaparte].—Who that?—He. There is an inscription to record this. Andernach—a fine entrance from Bemagne, with its massy towers and square-spired church. From Andernach we passed on. Saw on the other side Neuwied, a town owing its existence to the mere toleration of religion. It is the finest and [most] flourishing we have seen since

Ghent and Antwerp. We saw the tomb of Hoche at a distance; went to it. There was inscribed "The army of the Sambre and the Moselle to its general-in-chief Hoche." The reliefs are torn off, the marble slabs broken, and it is falling. But—

> "Glory of the fallen brave
> Shall men remember though forgot their grave,"

and the enemies may launch malicious darts against it. After Andernach the Rhine loses much. The valley is wider, and the beautiful, after the almost sublime, palls, and man is fastidious.

[The celebrated lyric by Byron introduced into *Childe Harold*, an address to his half-sister, is stated farther on to have been written on this very day. I cite the first stanza—

> "The castled crag of Drachenfels
> Frowns o'er the wide and winding Rhine,
> Whose breast of waters broadly swells
> Between the banks which bear the vine;
> And hills all rich with blossom'd trees,
> And fields which promise corn and wine,
> And scatter'd cities crowning these,
> Whose far white walls along them shine,
> Have strew'd a scene which I should see
> With double joy wert thou with me."]

About a mile from Coblentz we saw Marceau's tomb—too dark. Crossed the bridge over the Moselle, entered Coblentz; asked of military, no pass; went to inns, rascals. Went to the Trois Suisses—well served; fine view of Ehrenbreitstein fortress in sight. When French besieged it, Marceau was here at this inn, and the cannon-ball pierced it several times.—There were 84 French officers here, when they would not believe the Cossacks would pass; they had to fly as quick as horses could convey them, for the C[ossacks], getting into boats, made their horses swim

across. C[ossack]s rascals—ate and drank and never paid. The
general of them mean into the bargain; for he sent the waiter in
search of a louis he had never dropped, and went off.—A flying
bridge in face of me.

[Marceau died in 1796 of a wound received near Altenkirchen,
at the age of only twenty-seven. High honours were paid to his
remains both by his own army and by the Austrians whom he
had been combating. Polidori passes rapidly from the affair
of Marceau to that of eighty-four French officers and a body
of Cossacks: but it is clear that these two matters have no real
connexion: the latter must relate to 1815 or 1814. Byron devotes
to Marceau two stanzas of *Childe Harold*—

> "By Coblentz, on a rise of gentle ground,
> There is a small and simple pyramid
> Crowning the summit of the verdant mound.
> Beneath its base are heroes' ashes hid,
> Our enemy's: but let not that forbid
> Honour to Marceau; o'er whose early tomb
> Tears, big tears, gush'd from the rough soldier's lid,
> Lamenting and yet envying such a doom,
> Falling for France, whose rights he battled to resume.
> "Brief, brave, and glorious, was his young career," etc.

General Hoche, although a separate monument to him was
observed by Byron and Polidori, was in fact buried in the same
tomb with Marceau. He died at Wetzlar in 1797, aged twenty-
nine. It may be noticed that Byron (line 4) writes "heroes'," plural,
followed by "enemy's," singular. "Heroes'" must be intended
for both Marceau and Hoche, and I suspect that "enemy's" is a
misprint for "enemies'."]

May 12.—Got up. Looked at the fine view, and went to the
bath, which was at a maltster's—30 sous. Thence entered a
Catholic church—organ—children singing, which had a fine
effect. A copy of Rubens—lineal. Breakfasted.

Mounted a calèche, and went to Marceau's monument. The tomb of heroes made into a certain place very much expressed the flickering flame of fame. Thence to the Chartreuse: deserted, ruined, windowless, roofless, and tenantless—with another in sight in the same state. Plenty of reliefs on the roadside belonging to the Road to Calvary, an oratory on the hillside, where were many peasants bowing in reverence. Thence to the flying bridge managed by boats fastened in the stream with a rope, and by the rudder.

Saw a motley group of peasants with their head-dresses of gold and crimson or green with the steel pin. Cocked hat, blue coat and stockinged heroes with a fork. Officers, artillery-men, etc.; crosses given apparently with as profuse a hand to the soldiers as to the roadside.

Went to Ehrenbreitstein. Everything broken by gunpowder; immense masses of solid stone and mortar thrown fifty yards from their original situation; ruined walls, gateways, and halls—nothing perfect. Splendid views thence—Coblentz, Rhine, Moselle with its bridge, mountains, cultivation, vines, wilderness, everything below my feet. Mounted again. Passed the Rhine in a boat (rowed), looking very like the Otaheitan canoes. Into the carriage—set off. Scenes increasing in sublimity. The road raised from the side of the river without parapet: two precipices coming to the road headlong. Indeed the river reaches foot to foot—splendid, splendid, splendid. Saw the fort belonging once to Muhrfrey, where he raised customs, and resisted in consequence sixty cities. Arrived at St. Goar. At the first post saw the people in church; went to hear them sing—fine.

May 13.—Left St. Goar. Found scenery sublime to Bingen. Men with cocked hats and great buckles hacking at the vines. The scenery after Bingen gains in beauty what it loses in sublimity. Immense plain to the mounts, with the Rhine *in medio*, covered with trees, woods, and forests. Fine road to Mayence made by Nap[oleon]; his name has been erased from the inscription on the column commemorative of the work. Insolence of power!

Mayence a fine town, with a cathedral raised above it of red sandstone. Bavarians, Austrians, and Prussians, all in the town—belonging to all. The best town we have seen since Ghent.

[Mayence was at this date, locally, in the Grand Duchy of Hesse: but as a fortress it appertained to the German Confederation, and was garrisoned by Austrians, Prussians, and Hessians (hardly perhaps Bavarians)].

One of our postillions blew a horn. Saw yesterday a beautiful appearance—two rainbows, one on the top of trees where the colours of the foliage pierced the rainbow-hues.

Arrived at Mayence at 6-1/2. Saw along the Rhine many fine old castles. This below is what L[ord] B[yron] wrote to Mrs. L[eigh] some days ago: written May 11 on Rhine-banks. See *Childe Harold*, from "The Castled Crag of Drachenfels" to "Still sweeten more these Banks of Rhine."[5]

May 14.—From Mayence, where I saw the spot where they said lately stood the house where printing was invented; it had been pulled down by the French. The gallery I could not see, because the keeper had taken it into his head to make a promenade. Saw the cathedral, pierced at the roof by bombs in the last siege the town underwent. The reliefs—some of which were in a good style—many decapitated. There was a German marshal who was represented as gravely putting forth his powdered head from under a tombstone he has just lifted up—with an inscription saying "I am here."

From Mayence we went to Mannheim through a fine country. Crossed the Rhine on a bridge of boats. Taken very ill with a fever at Mannheim—could not write my Journal.

May 15.—Being a little recovered, set off. Fine alleys of Lombardy-poplars and horse-chestnuts—neat villages. Entered Carlsruhe through a grove of Scotch firs and other trees that had a fine effect. Saw the Palace.

Entered the inn, and was very ill. Took ipecac and op. gr. 15. Headache, vertigo, tendency to fainting, etc. Magnesia and lemon acid—a little better, no effect.

Went a drive about the town. Saw the neatest town we have yet met with: the only objection is the houses stuccoed white—bad for the eyes. Saw the outside of the Palace, and went into the garden laid out in the English manner.

Went home: dreadful headaches: ate some stewed apples; took some more magn[esia] and acid; had no effect; lay down; got up after two hours. Was just going out when L[ord] B[yron] came to take from my hand a plated candlestick, to give me a brass one. Got on a few steps; fainted. My fall brought the servants to me. Took 4 pills; going out again, when L[ord] B[yron] made the servant put down the plated candlestick, to take up a brass one; went to bed.

[This, as Polidori evidently thought, was an odd incident, not easily accounted for. One cannot suppose that Byron simply aimed at humiliating or mortifying his physician. There must have been a candle in each candlestick; and it is conceivable that the candle in the brass one was the longer, and therefore the more suitable for an invalid who might have needed it throughout the night.]

Medicine had violent effect: better on the whole, though weak.

Just as we were going out I met Sir C. Hunter at my chamber-door, who told me he had heard so bad an account of my positively dying that he came to enquire how I found myself. I asked him in. He took care to tell us he was a great friend of the Grand Duke, who had sent his groom of the stole (he called it stool) in search of lodgings for the worthy Mayor;[6] gave us a long sermon about rheumatism, routes, etc.; left us. In the evening he sent in the *Guide du Voyageur en les pays de l'Europe*, begging in return some of L[ord] B[yron's] poems.

Went out. Saw a church. Columns like firs—Corinthian, golden capitals: loaded everywhere with gilt, perhaps tawdry, but fine-tawdry. The environs are beautiful. Drove a great deal about: fine trees and fine cultivation.

May 18.—From Carlsruhe to Offenberg; much better. Slept halfway: blinds down the other, so nothing to mention except fine trees, fine cocked hats, fine women, and yellow-coated postillions.

May 19.—Set off from Offenberg; saw some scenes that pleased me much; hills and clouds upon them; woods with mists. Passed through Freiburg, where we saw the steeple pervious to the top with trellis-work showing the light, which had to my eyes a beautiful appearance.

I think Charles, when he said, "The German for his horse," remembered the G[erman] postillions; for they talk to theirs, and the horses on their part listen and seem to understand. The greater part of to-day I have found the ladies in a strange costume of short wide red petticoats with many folds, and a hat of straw as wide as a wheel. Arrived at Krolzingen to sleep. Left Krolzingen: got to a hill. Fine view thence: the Alps, the Rhine, the Jura mountains, and a fine plain before us—fine country. Crossed the Rhine, and were in Switzerland. The town upon unequal ground—some parts very high, and some low; the greater part very narrow streets. After tea went to take a walk: went upon the Rhine bridge—upon a hill in the town [Bâle presumably].

May 21.—Went to see a panorama of Thun, the first Swiss one: crowded foolishly with people, and too small. Saw a gallery that the artist had formed. A fine Raphael, not his; a good Rembrandt, the first I saw historical; a *Circumcision*; a head of the caricaturist David; two heads of Divinity; a *Christ and Virgin*—mere pieces of flesh and drapery. Went to a marchand d'estampes. Saw there *Nelson's Death*, Chatham's ditto, and other pictures of England. *The Dance of Death* has been destroyed: but it was not Holbein's, but his restorer's. The collection is dispersed, that once was here, of his paintings.

Agreed with a voiturier to take our carriages to Geneva in five days. Set off. Country increases from hills to mountains with great beauty. Passed through Lipstadt and came to ——. Went before supper to climb a hill where we found a goatherd who could not understand the French that asked for milk till it had the commentary, "We will pay for it." The scene was very fine: to the

67

right, beautiful; to the left, it had a tendency to sublimity; on one side, hills covered to the top with trees; on the other, mountains with bald pates. Came down. Found the servants playing at bowls. They were obliged to run the bowls along a narrow board to the men. Supper: read *Arabian Nights*; went to bed.

May 22.—Left —— at 9; passed the Jura mountains, where we saw some fine castellated scenery, and women ornamented strangely—amazingly short petticoats, not below the knee, with black crape rays round their heads that make them look very spidery. Soleure is a neat town with stone fortifications, and a clean church with fountains before it. The houses in this neighbourhood have a pleasing strange appearance on account of the roofs, which slant out on every side a great way. Immense number of Scotch firs—roads fine. Voituriers slow, and have eight francs of drink-money a day, being two; which being too much according to the *Guide du Voyageur en Europe*, where it is said 1-1/2 fr., we showed it to our courier, who was in a passion. Came to ——, where we slept.

May 23.—Left ——: got a sight of some fine Alpine snow-capped mountains. Came to Berne; delightfully situated; beautiful streets with arcades all their length. Dined there. Saw a splendidly beautiful view coming down a hill, with hills covered with fir, ash, beech, and all the catalogue of trees; Morat at the bottom, and the Jura mounts behind, with snowy hair and cloudy night-caps. Arrived at Morat; neat with arcades. Stopped at the Crown inn. All the way had debates whether clouds were mountains, or mountains clouds.

May 24.—The innkeeper at Morat, being a little tipsy, and thinking every Englishman (being a philosophe) must be a philosophe like himself, favoured us with some of his infidel notions while serving us at supper. Near Morat was fought the battle wherein the Burgundians were so completely thrashed. Their bones, of which we took pieces, are now very few; once they formed a mighty heap in the chapel, but both were destroyed by the Burgundian division when in Switzerland, and a tree of liberty was planted over it, which yet flourishes in all its verdure—the liberty has flown from the planters' grasp. Saw Aventicum; there remains sufficient of the walls to trace the boundaries of the ancient town; but of all the buildings, both for Gods and men, nothing but a column remains, and that the only remnant for more than a hundred years. There are mosaic pavements, and even the streets may be perceived in a dry summer by the grass being thinner. The mosaic in a barn, probably once of a temple, was pretty perfect till the Gallic cavalry came and turned it into a stable. It is formed of little pieces of black, white, and red bricks; little now remains. There was also a copper vessel in the middle; that too has disappeared. The town is shamefully negligent of the antiquities of their fathers, for there is another more beautiful and perfect mosaic pavement discovered, but which they have allowed the proprietor to cover again with mould rather than buy it. We found in a barn heads, plinths, capitals, and shafts, heaped promiscuously. The Corinthian-column capital is deeply, sharply, and beautifully cut. A head of Apollo in all the rudeness of first art—a capital of a strange mixed order. There is the Amphitheatre, hollow yet pretty perfect, but no stonework visible; overgrown with trees; the size, my companion told me, was larger than common. In the town there were some beautiful fragments of ornament-sculpture incorporated in the walls; all marble. In the walls of the church we sought in vain for the inscription that Mathison mentions to Julia Alpinula.

[Both to Morat and to Aventicum (Avenches) Byron devotes some stanzas in *Childe Harold*, 63 to 67, and notes to correspond. Morat he terms "the proud, the patriot field." He speaks of the hoard of bones, and says: "I ventured to bring away as much as may have made a quarter of a hero," for "careful preservation." His reference to Aventicum and the inscription to Julia Alpinula reads rather curiously in the light of Polidori's avowal that "we sought in vain for the inscription." Byron's readers must always, I apprehend, have inferred the contrary.

"By a lone wall a lonelier column rears
A grey and grief-worn aspect of old days.
'Tis the last remnant of the wreck of years,
And looks as with the wild bewildered gaze
Of one to stone converted by amaze,
Yet still with consciousness: and there it stands,
Making a marvel that it not decays,
When the coeval pride of human hands,
Levell'd Aventicum, hath strew'd her subject lands.

"And there—oh sweet and sacred be the name!—
Julia, the daughter, the devoted, gave
Her youth to Heaven: her heart, beneath a claim
Nearest to Heaven's, broke o'er a father's grave.
Justice is sworn 'gainst tears; and hers would crave
The life she lived in; but the judge was just,—
And then she died on him she could not save.
Their tomb was simple, and without a bust,
And held within their urn one mind, one heart, one dust."

Byron's note runs thus: "Julia Alpinula, a young Aventian priestess, died soon after a vain endeavour to save her father, condemned to death as a traitor by Aulus Cæcina. Her epitaph was discovered many years ago. It is thus: 'Julia Alpinula hic jaceo. Infelicis patris infelix proles. Deæ Aventiæ Sacerdos. Exorare patris necem non potui: Male mori in fatis illi erat. Vixi annos XXIII.' I know of no human composition so affecting as this, nor a history of greater interest. These are the names and actions," etc.]

I copied the one below on account of its medical tendency. The letters in this as well as in all the other inscriptions are formed like our Roman print, not in the least imperfect: "Nvminib. Avg. et Genio Col. I. El. Apollini Sagr. 9. Postum Hermes lib. Medicis et Professorib, D.S.D."

From Aventicum or Avenches we went to Payerne. We have

seen in many places boys leading goats just in the antique style. Thence we went to Moudon—dirty town. Stopped for refreshments. One fine view we have had all the way, but nothing equal to the view descending to Morat.

Darkness came on. We saw the Castle wherein —— defended himself against the French who besieged it for a month: looks so weak, it seems a wonder. The Swiss castles are not nearly so interesting as the Rhine ones. They are very conical-roofed and no battlements. We saw the lake, but for a long time doubted whether it was a cloud below, a mist before, or water beneath us. Entered Lausanne.

May 25.—Left Lausanne, after having looked at a bookseller's, who showed me a fine collection of bad books for four louis. Enquired for Dewar: name not known. We went along the lake, that a little disappointed me, as it does not seem so broad as it really is, and the mountains near it, though covered with snow, have not a great appearance on account of the height [of the] lake itself. We saw Mont Blanc in the distance; ethereal in appearance, mingling with the clouds; it is more than 60 miles from where we saw it. It is a classic ground we go over. Buonaparte, Joseph, Bonnet, Necker, Staël, Voltaire, Rousseau, all have their villas (except Rousseau). Genthoud, Ferney, Coppet, are close to the road.

[Perhaps some readers may need to be reminded who Bonnet was. He was a great physicist, both practical and speculative, Charles Bonnet, author of a *Traité d'Insectologie*, a *Traité de l'usage des Feuilles*, *Contemplations de la Nature*, *Palingénésie Philosophique*, and other works. Born in Geneva in 1720, he died in 1793.]

We arrived at Sécheron—where Lord Byron, having put his age down as 100, received a letter half-an-hour after from Inn Keeper?—a thing that seems worthy of a novel. It begins again to be the land of the vine. Women, who till the Pays de Vaud were ugly, improving greatly.

May 26.—After breakfast, and having made up the accounts

to to-day, and having heard that the voituriers made a claim of drink-money all the way back, we ordered a calèche; but, happening to go into the garden, we saw a boat, into which entering, we pushed out upon the Leman Lake. After rowing some time, happening to come to the ferry, we found the waiter with a direful look to tell us that it was*pris pour un monsieur Anglais*, who happened to be ——.[7] We got another, and went out to bathe. I *rode* first with L[ord] B[yron] upon the field of Waterloo; *walked* first to see Churchill's tomb; *bathed and rowed* first on the Leman Lake.—It did us much good. Dined; entered the calèche; drove through Geneva, where I saw an effect of building that pleased me: it was porticoes from the very roof of the high houses to the bottom.

Went to the house beyond Cologny that belonged to Diodati. They ask five-and-twenty louis for it a month. Narrow, not true. The view from his house is very fine; beautiful lake; at the bottom of the crescent is Geneva. Returned. Pictet called, but L[ord] B[yron] said "not at home."

[There were two Genevan Pictets at this date, both public men of some mark. One was Jean Marc Jules Pictet de Sergy, 1768 to 1828; the other, the Chevalier Marc Auguste Pictet, 1752 to 1825. As Polidori speaks farther on of Pictet as being aged about forty-six, the former would appear to be meant. He had been in Napoleon's legislative chamber from 1800 to 1815, and was afterwards a member of the representative council of Geneva.— The Villa Diodati was the house where Milton, in 1639, had visited Dr. John Diodati, a Genevese Professor of Theology. Polidori's compact phrase, "narrow, not true," is by no means clear; perhaps he means that some one had warned him that the Villa Diodati (called also the Villa Belle Rive) was inconveniently narrow, but, on inspecting the premises, he found the statement incorrect.]

May 27.—Got up; went about a boat; got one for 3 fr. a day; rowed to Sécheron. Breakfasted. Got into a carriage. Went to Banker's, who changed our money, and afterwards left his card. To Pictet—not at home. Home, and looked at accounts: bad temper on my side. Went into the boat, rowed across to Diodati; cannot have it for three years; English family. Crossed again; I went; L[ord] B[yron] back. Getting out, L[ord] B[yron] met M[ary] Wollstonecraft Godwin, her sister, and Percy Shelley. I got into the boat into the middle of Leman Lake, and there lay my length, letting the boat go its way.

[Here I find it difficult to understand the phrase—"Cannot have it (Villa Diodati) for three years—English family." It must apparently mean either that an English family were occupying or had bespoken Villa Diodati, and would remain there for three years to come (which is in conflict with the fact that Byron soon afterwards became the tenant); or else that Byron thought of renting it for a term as long as three years, which was barred by the previous claim of some English family. On the whole, the latter supposition seems to me the more feasible; but one is surprised to think that Byron had any—even remote—idea of remaining near Geneva for any such great length of time. This sets one's mind speculating about Miss Clairmont, with whom (as is well known) Byron's amour had begun before he left London, and who had now just arrived to join him at Sécheron; had he at this time any notion of settling down with her in the neighbourhood for three years, more or less? It is a curious point to consider for us who know how rapidly he discarded her, and how harshly he treated her ever afterwards. Miss Clairmont, we see, was now already on the spot, along with Percy and Mary Shelley; in fact, as we learn from other sources, they had arrived at Sécheron, Dejean's Hôtel de l'Angleterre, as far back as May 18, or perhaps May 15—and Byron now for the first time encountered the three. It appears that he must have met Mary Godwin in London, probably only once—not to speak of Clare. Shelley, to the best of our information, he had never till now seen at all. Polidori here terms Clare Clairmont the "sister" of "M. Wollstonecraft Godwin"; and in the entry for May 29 he even applies the name Wollstonecraft Godwin to Clare; and it will be found as we proceed that for some little while he really supposed the two ladies to be sisters in the right sense of the term, both of them bearing the surname of Godwin. In point of fact, there was no blood-relationship—Mary being the daughter of Mr. and the first Mrs. Godwin, and Clare the daughter of Mr. and Mrs. Clairmont. It may be as well to add that the letters addressed by Miss Clairmont to Byron, before they actually met in London, have now (1904) been published in *The Works of Lord Byron, Letters and Journals*, vol. iii, pp. 429-437; and they certainly exhibit a degree of forwardness and importunity which accounts in some measure for his eventual antipathy to her.]

Found letter from De Roche inviting me to breakfast to-morrow; curious with regard to L[ord] B[yron]. Dined; P[ercy] S[helley], the author of *Queen Mab*, came; bashful, shy, consumptive; twenty-six; separated from his wife; keeps the two daughters of Godwin, who practise his theories; one L[ord] B[yron]'s.

[This is a very noticeable jotting. Shelley appears to have come in alone on this occasion, and we may infer that some very confidential talk ensued between him and Byron, in the presence of Polidori. He was not at this date really twenty-six years of age, but only twenty-three. "Bashful, shy," is an amusingly simple description of him. As to "consumptive," we know that Shelley left England under the impression that consumption had him in its grip, but this hardly appears to have been truly the case. Polidori, as a medical man, might have been expected to express some doubt on the subject, unless the poet's outward appearance looked consumptive. Next we hear that Shelley "keeps the two daughters of Godwin, who practise his theories"—*i.e.* set the marriage-laws at defiance, or act upon the principle of free love. One might suppose, from this phrase, that Polidori believed Shelley to be the accepted lover of Miss Clairmont as well as of Mary Godwin; but the addition of those very significant words— "One, Lord Byron's"—tells in the opposite direction. These words can only mean (what was the fact) that one of these ladies, viz. Miss Clairmont, was Lord Byron's mistress. Therefore Polidori, in saying that Shelley "kept the two daughters of Godwin," may presumably have meant that he housed and maintained Clare, while he was the *quasi*-husband of Mary. Whether Polidori now for the first time learned, from the conversation of Byron and Shelley, what was the relation subsisting between Clare and Byron, or whether Byron had at some earlier date imparted the facts to him, is a question which must remain unsolved. The latter appears to me extremely probable; for Byron had certainly arranged to meet Clare near Geneva, and he may very likely have given the requisite notice beforehand to his travelling physician and daily associate. My aunt Charlotte Polidori was not an adept in Shelleian detail: if she had been, I fear that these sentences would have shocked her sense of propriety, and they would have been left uncopied. They form the only passage in her transcript which bears in any way upon the amour between Lord Byron and Miss Clairmont; to the best of my recollection and belief there was not in the original Diary any other passage pointing in the same direction.—I may observe here that there is nothing in Polidori's Journal to show that the Shelley party were staying in the same Sécheron hotel with Lord Byron. Professor Dowden says that they were—I suppose with some sufficient authority; and I think other biographers in general have assumed the same.]

Into the calèche; horloger's at Geneva; L[ord] B[yron] paid 15 nap. towards a watch; I, 13: repeater and minute-hand; foolish watch.

[This means (as one of Polidori's letters shows) that Byron made him a present of £15 towards the price of the watch.]

Went to see the house of Madame Necker, 100 a half-year; came home, etc.

May 28.—Went to Geneva, to breakfast with Dr. De Roche; acute, sensible, a listener to himself; good clear head. Told me that armies on their march induce a fever (by their accumulation of animal dirt, irregular regimen) of the most malignant typhoid kind; it is epidemic. There was a whole feverish line from Moscow to Metz, and it spread at Geneva the only almost epidemic typhus for many years. He is occupied in the erection of Lancaster schools, which he says succeed well. He is a Louis Bourbonist. He told me my fever was not an uncommon one among travellers. He came home with me, and we had a chat with L[ord] B[yron]; chiefly politics, where of course we differed. He had a system well worked out, but I hope only hypothetical, about liberty of the French being Machiavellianly not desirable by Europe. He pointed out Dumont in the court, the rédacteur of Bentham.

Found a letter from Necker to the hotel-master, asking 100 nap. for three months; and another from Pictet inviting L[ord] B[yron] and any friend to go with him at 8 to Madame Einard, a connection of his. We then, ascending our car, went to see some other houses, none suiting.

When we returned home, Mr. Percy Shelley came in to ask us to dinner; declined; engaged for tomorrow. We walked with him, and got into his boat, though the wind raised a little sea upon the lake. Dined at four. Mr. Hentsch, the banker, came in; very polite; told L[ord] B[yron] that, when he saw him yesterday, he had not an idea that he was speaking to one of the most famous lords of England.

Dressed and went to Pictet's: an oldish man, about forty-six, tall, well-looking, speaks English well. His daughter showed us a picture, by a young female artist, of Madame Lavallière in the chapel; well executed in pencil—good lights and a lusciously grieving expression.

Went to Madame Einard. Introduced to a room where about 8 (afterwards 20), 2 ladies (1 more). L[ord] B[yron]'s name was alone mentioned; mine, like a star in the halo of the moon, invisible. L[ord] B[yron] not speaking French, M. Einard spoke bad Italian. A Signor Rossi came in, who had joined Murat at Bologna. Manly in thought; admired Dante as a poet more than Ariosto, and a discussion about manliness in a language. Told me Geneva women amazingly chaste even in thoughts. Saw the Lavallière artist. A bonny, rosy, seventy-yeared man, called Bonstetten, the beloved of Gray and the correspondent of Mathison.

[I find "40" in the MS.: apparently it ought to be "70," for Bonstetten was born in 1745. He lived on till 1832. Charles Victor de Bonstetten was a Bernese nobleman who had gone through various vicissitudes of opinion and adventure, travelling in England and elsewhere. To Englishmen (as indicated in Polidori's remark) he is best known as a friend of the poet Thomas Gray, whom he met in 1769. He said: "Jamais je n'ai vu personne qui donnât autant que Gray l'idée d'un gentleman accompli." Among the chief writings of Bonstetten are *Recherches sur la Nature et les Lois de l'Imagination*; *Etudes d'Hommes*; *L'Homme du Midi et l'Homme du Nord*.]

Madame Einard made tea, and left all to take sugar with the fingers. Madame Einard showed some historical pieces of her doing in acquerella, really good, a little too French-gracish. Obliged to leave before ten for the gates shut. Came home, went to bed.

Was introduced by Shelley to Mary Wollstonecraft Godwin, called here Mrs. Shelley. Saw picture by Madame Einard of a cave in the Jura where in winter there is no ice, in summer plenty. No names announced, no ceremony—each speaks to whom he pleases. Saw the bust of Jean Jacques erected upon the spot where the Geneva magistrates were shot. L[ord] B[yron] said it was probably built of some of the stones with which they pelted him.[8] The walk is deserted. They are now mending their roads. Formerly they could not, because the municipal money always went to the public box.

May 29.—Went with Mr. Hentsch to see some houses along the valley in which runs the Rhone: nothing. Dined with Mr. and Mrs. Percy Shelley and Wollstonecraft Godwin. Hentsch told us that the English last year exported corn to Italy to a great amount.

May 30.—Got up late. Went to Mr. and Mrs. Shelley; breakfasted with them; rowed out to see a house together. S[helley] went from Lucerne with the two, with merely £26, to England along the Rhine in bateaux. Gone through much misery, thinking he was dying; married a girl for the mere sake of letting her have the jointure that would accrue to her; recovered; found he could not agree; separated; paid Godwin's debts, and seduced his daughter; then wondered that he would not see him. The sister left the father to go with the other. Got a child. All clever, and no meretricious appearance. He is very clever; the more I read his *Queen Mab*, the more beauties I find. Published at fourteen a novel; got £30 for it; by his second work £100. *Mab* not published.—Went in calèche with L[ord] B[yron] to see a house; again after dinner to leave cards; then on lake with L[ord] B[yron]. I, Mrs. S[helley], and Miss G[odwin], on to the lake till nine. Drank tea, and came away at 11 after confabbing. The batelier went to Shelley, and asked him as a favour not to tell L[ord] B[yron] what he gave for his boat, as he thought it quite fit that Milord's payment be double; we sent Berger to say we did not wish for the boat.

[The statement that "Shelley went from Lucerne with the two, with merely £26, to England, along the Rhine in bateaux," refers of course to what had taken place in 1814, on the occasion of Shelley's elopement with Mary Godwin, and has no bearing on the transactions of 1816; it must be cited by Polidori as showing how inexpensively three persons could, if so minded, travel from Switzerland to England. The other references to Shelley's domestic affairs etc. are very curious. Except as to his own personal admiration for *Queen Mab*, Polidori is here evidently putting down (but not in the words of Shelley himself, who would assuredly not have said that he had "seduced" Mary Godwin) such details as the poet imparted to him. They are far from accurate. To some extent, Polidori may have remembered imperfectly what Shelley told him, but I think the latter must have been responsible for most of the fables; and generally it would appear that Shelley gave free rein to his inclination for romancing or for over-stating matters, possibly perceiving that Polidori was credulous, and capable of swallowing whatever he was told, the more eccentric the better. To say that Shelley, before he, at the age of barely 19, married Harriet Westbrook in 1811, thought that he was dying, and that his only practical motive for marrying her was that she might come in for a jointure after his decease, is no doubt highly fallacious, and even absurd. We have other sources of information as to these occurrences, especially the letters of Shelley addressed at the time to Jefferson Hogg, and they tell a very different tale. As to his reason for separating from Harriet, Shelley, we perceive, simply told Polidori that he "found he could not agree" with her; he said nothing as to his knowing or supposing that she had been unfaithful to him. Again, Shelley was not so boyish as 14 when he published a novel—his first novel, the egregious *Zastrozzi*; the publication took place in 1810, when he was eighteen, or at lowest seventeen. The statement that he got £100 by "his second work" is worth considering. If "his second work" means, as one might naturally suppose in this connexion, the romance of *St. Irvyne*, the suggestion that he got anything at all by it, except a state of indebtedness, is a novelty. But our mind recurs to that rumoured and apparently really published though wholly untraced work of his, *A Poetical Essay on the Existing State of Things*. This poem was published, we are told, for the benefit of an Irish agitator or patriot, Peter Finnerty, and it has been elsewhere averred that the publication produced a sum of nearly £100. The mention by Polidori of £100 may be surmised to refer to the same matter, and it tends so far to confirm the idea that the book really existed, and even secured a fair measure of success.—Berger (who is named in connexion with Byron and the hire for the boat) was, as already noted, the Swiss servant of Byron, brought from London.]

May 31.—Breakfasted with Shelley; read Italian with Mrs. S[helley]; dined; went into a boat with Mrs. S[helley], and rowed all night till 9; tea'd together; chatted, etc.

June 1.—Breakfasted with S[helley]; entered a calèche; took Necker's house for 100 louis for 8 or 365 days. Saw several houses for Shelley; one good. Dined; went in the boat; all tea'd together.

[Necker's house, here mentioned, would apparently be the same as the Villa Diodati, or Villa Belle Rive—for that is the house which Byron did in fact rent. "Necker" may be understood as meaning (rather than the famous Minister of Finance in France) his widow, since Necker himself had died a dozen years before. The sum of 100 louis seems to be specified here as the rent for a year, and the phrase about 8 days must indicate that the house could be tenanted for that short space of time— or let us say a week—at a proportionate payment. This rate of rental appears low, and it differs both from what was said under the date of May 26, and from what we shall find noted shortly afterwards, June 6. Thus I feel a little doubt whether "Necker's house" is not in reality something quite different from the Villa Diodati. Byron's proposed tenancy of the former might possibly have been cancelled.]

Rogers the subject: L[or]d B[yron] thinks good poet; malicious. Marquis of Lansdowne being praised by a whole company as a happy man, having all good, R[ogers] said, "But how horridly he carves turbot!" Ward having reviewed his poems in the *Quarterly*, having a bad heart and being accused of learning his speeches, L[ord] B[yron], upon malignantly hinting to him [Rogers] how he had been carved, heard him say: "I stopped his speaking though by my epigram, which is—

"'Ward has no heart, they say, but I deny it;
He has a heart, and gets his speeches by it.'"

[This must be the Honourable John William Ward, who was created Earl of Dudley in 1827, and died in 1833. Miss Berry, the *quasi*-adopted daughter of Horace Walpole, told Madame de Staël in 1813 that the latter had "undertaken two miracles—to make Ward *poli envers les femmes et pieux envers Dieu*."]

On L[ord] B[yron's] writing a poem to his sister wherein he says, "And when friends e'en paused and love," etc., Rogers, going to some one, said: "I don't know what L[ord] B[yron] means by *pausing*; I called upon him every day." He did this regularly, telling L[ord] B[yron] all the bad news with a malignant grin. When L[ord] B[yron] wrote "Weep, daughter of a royal line," Rogers came to him one day, and, taking up the *Courier*, said: "I am sure now you're attacked there; now don't mind them"; and began reading, looking every now and then at L[ord] B[yron] with an anxious searching eye, till he came to "that little poet and disagreeable person, Mr. Samuel—" when he tore the paper, and said: "Now this must be that fellow Croker," and wished L[ord] B[yron] to challenge him. He talked of going to Cumberland with L[ord] B[yron], and, asking him how he meant to travel, L[ord] B[yron] said "With four horses." Rogers went to company, and said: "It is strange to hear a man talking of four horses who seals his letters with a tallow candle."

Shelley is another instance of wealth inducing relations to confine for madness, and was only saved by his physician being honest. He was betrothed from a boy to his cousin, for age; another came who had as much as he *would* have, and she left him "because he was an atheist." When starving, a friend to whom he had given £2000, though he knew it, would not come near him. Heard Mrs. Shelley repeat Coleridge on Pitt, which persuades me he is a poet.

[Here we see that Shelley must have repeated to Polidori that famous story of his about the attempt of his father to consign him, when he was an Eton student, to a madhouse, and about the zealous and ultimately successful effort of Dr. Lind, the Eton physicist, to save him from that disastrous fate. Next comes the statement that Shelley was betrothed from boyhood to his beautiful cousin Miss Harriet Grove—the marriage to take effect when he should attain his majority; an account which we know to be substantially true. The conduct of Miss Grove—or perhaps we should rather say of her parents as dictating her action—is placed in an unfavourable light; for it is plainly suggested that she abandoned Shelley for another bridegroom on the ground of a more immediate advantage in worldly position—the allegation of Percy's atheism being more a pretext than a genuine motive. The passage about a friend to whom Shelley had given £2000 must (I suppose beyond a doubt) refer to Godwin; but it is evident that Shelley, in speaking to Polidori, a comparative stranger, and this in the presence of Mary, had the delicacy to suppress the name. The charge thus alleged against Godwin is not, I conceive, accurate, although it approximated towards accuracy. I am not clear that Shelley, up to the time when he thus spoke in June 1816, had given Godwin money amounting to quite so large a total as £2000; but at any rate he cannot have done so up to the time when he was himself "starving"— or, in milder terms, when he was in very great and harassing straits for money and daily subsistence. That time was late in 1814, and in the first days of 1815. It is true that, even before this date, he had done something to relieve Godwin; but it was only, I think, in April 1816 that he gave the philosopher a really very considerable sum—£1000 in a lump. I say all this for the sake of biographical truth, and not with a view to vindicating Godwin—whose policy of bleeding Shelley in purse while he cut him in person has in some recent years been denounced with increasing vehemence, and it was indeed wholly indefensible. But human nature—and especially the human nature of an abstract speculator like Godwin—is capable of very odd self-deceptions; and I dare say Godwin thought he was equally and strictly right in both his proceedings—right in getting large sums of money out of Shelley, for a reforming sage ought to be subsidized by his neophytes—and right in repudiating and abusing Shelley, for the latter had applied Godwin's own anti-matrimonial theories to that one instance of practice which the philosopher did not at all relish.—To proceed to another point. The lines of Coleridge on Pitt which Polidori heard recited by Mrs. Shelley are to be sought for in his early poem entitled *Fire, Famine, and Slaughter*. In that poem (need I say it?) those three Infernal Deities are represented as meeting in "a desolated tract in La Vendée"; and on mutual enquiry they learn that one and the same person has sent them thither all three.

"Letters four do form his name"—

the name Pitt. Famine and Slaughter finally agree that the multitude, exasperated by their sufferings, shall turn upon Pitt and rend him—

"They shall tear him limb from limb!"

Fire, who has just come from doing Pitt's errands in Ireland, thinks this ungrateful: she concludes the poem with the memorable words—

"Ninety months he, by my troth,
Hath richly catered for you both:
And in an hour would you repay
An eight years' work?—Away, away!
I alone am faithful—*I*
Cling to him everlastingly."

The poem would be well worth quoting here in full, but is somewhat too long for such a purpose.]

A young girl of eighteen, handsome, died within half-an-hour yesterday: buried to-day. Geneva is fortified—legumes growing in the fosses.—Went about linen and plate.

June 2.—Breakfasted with Shelley. Read Tasso with Mrs. Shelley. Took child for vaccination.

[The child in question must seemingly have been the beloved infant William Shelley, born in January of this same year. Polidori does not appear to have vaccinated the boy with his own hand; for I find in a letter of his written to his family towards June 20: "Got a gold chain and a seal as a fee from an Englishman here for having his child inoculated." As Polidori speaks only of "an Englishman here," not naming Shelley, it looks as if he purposely withheld from his family the knowledge that he had come into contact with that wicked and dangerous character. I wish I knew what has become of the "gold chain and seal," the gift of Shelley: but I could not on enquiry find that anything whatever was known about them by my then surviving relatives. I possess a letter on the subject, November 4, 1890, from my sister Christina.]

Found gates shut because of church-service. Went in search of Rossi. Saw a village where lads and lasses, soubrettes and soldiers, were dancing, to a tabor and drum, waltzes, cotillions, etc. Dr. R[ossi] not at home.

Dined with S[helley]; went to the lake with them and L[ord] B[yron]. Saw their house; fine. Coming back, the sunset, the mountains on one side, a dark mass of outline on the other, trees, houses hardly visible, just distinguishable; a white light mist, resting on the hills around, formed the blue into a circular dome bespangled with stars only and lighted by the moon which gilt the lake. The dome of heaven seemed oval. At 10 landed and drank tea. Madness, Grattan, Curran, etc., subjects.

[The "house" of Shelley and his party which is here mentioned is the Campagne Chapuis, or Campagne Mont Alègre, near Cologny—distant from the Villa Diodati only about 8 minutes' walk. Shelley and the two ladies had entered this house towards the end of May, prior to the actual settlement of Lord Byron in the Villa Diodati. The Shelleys, as we have more than once heard from this Diary, kept up the practice of drinking tea—a beverage always cherished by Percy Bysshe. The topics of conversation, we observe, were madness—probably following on from what Shelley had on the previous day said about his own supposed madness while at Eton; also Curran, whom Shelley had seen a little, but without any sympathy, in Dublin—and Grattan, who, so far as I am aware was not personally known to the poet.]

June 3.—Went to Pictet's on English day.

June 4.—Went about Diodati's house. Then to see Shelley, who, with Mrs. Shelley, came over. Went in the evening to a musical society of about ten members at M. Odier's; who read a very interesting memoir upon the subject of whether a physician should in any case tell a lover the health [of the lady of his affections], or anything that, from being her physician, comes to his knowledge. Afterwards had tea and politics. Saw there a Dr. Gardner, whom I carried home in the calèche. Odier invited me for every Wednesday.

Came home. Went on the lake with Shelley and Lord Byron, who quarrelled with me.

[This might seem to be the matter to which Professor Dowden in his *Life of Shelley* (following Moore's *Life of Byron* and some other authorities) thus briefly refers. "Towards Shelley the Doctor's feeling was a constantly self-vexing jealousy [I cannot say that the Diary of Polidori has up to this point borne the least trace of any such soreness]; and on one occasion, suffering from the cruel wrong of having been a loser in a sailing-match, he went so far as to send Shelley a challenge, which was received with a fit of becoming laughter. 'Recollect,' said Byron, 'that, though Shelley has some scruples about duelling, I have none and shall be at all times ready to take his place.'" Professor Dowden does not define the date when this squabble occurred; but the context in which he sets it suggests a date anterior to June 22, when Byron and Shelley started off on their week's excursion upon the Lake of Geneva. The very curt narrative of Polidori does not however indicate any sailing-match, nor any challenge, whether "sent" or verbally delivered at the moment; and perhaps it may be more reasonable to suppose that this present quarrel with Byron was a different affair altogether—an instance when Polidori happened to strike Byron's knee with an oar. I shall recur to the duelling matter farther on.]

June 5.—At 12 went to Hentsch about Diodati; thence to Shelley's. Read Tasso. Home in calèche. Dined with them in the public room: walked in the garden. Then dressed, and to Odier's, who talked with me about somnambulism. Was at last seated, and conversed with some Génevoises: so so—too fine.

Quantities of English; speaking amongst themselves, arms by their sides, mouths open and eyes glowing; might as well make a tour of the Isle of Dogs. Odier gave me yesterday many articles of *Bibliothèque*—translated and *rédigés* by himself, and to-day a manuscript on somnambulism.

[After the word *Bibliothèque* Charlotte Polidori has put some other word, evidently intended to imitate the *look* of the word written by Dr. Polidori: it cannot be read. The subject of somnambulism was one which had engaged Polidori's attention at an early age: he printed in 1815 a *Disputatio Medica Inauguralis de Oneirodyniâ*, as a thesis for the medical degree which he then obtained in Edinburgh.]

June 6.—At 1 up—breakfasted. With Lord Byron in the calèche to Hentsch, where we got the paper making us masters of Diodati for six months to November 1 for 125 louis.

[See my remarks under June 1 as to "Necker's house," and the rent to be paid. Up to November 1 would be barely five months, not six.]

Thence to Shelley: back: dinner. To Shelley in boat: driven on shore: home. Looked over inventory and Berger's accounts. Bed.

June 7.—Up at ——. Pains in my loins and languor in my bones. Breakfasted—looked over inventory.

Saw L[ord] B[yron] at dinner; wrote to my father and Shelley; went in the boat with L[ord] B[yron]; agreed with boatman for English boat. Told us Napoleon had caused him to get his children. Saw Shelley over again.

[It seems rather curious that Polidori, living so near Shelley, should now have had occasion to write to him; ought we to infer that the challenge was now at last sent? Perhaps so; and perhaps, when Polidori "saw Shelley over again," the poet laughed the whole foolish matter off.—The boatman's statement that "Napoleon had caused him to get his children" means, I suppose, that he wanted to rear children, to meet Napoleon's conscriptions for soldiers.]

June 8.—Up at 9; went to Geneva on horseback, and then to Diodati to see Shelley; back; dined; into the new boat—Shelley's,—

and talked, till the ladies' brains whizzed with giddiness, about idealism. Back; rain; puffs of wind. Mistake.

June 9.—Up by 1: breakfasted. Read Lucian. Dined. Did the same: tea'd. Went to Hentsch: came home. Looked at the moon, and ordered packing-up.

June 10.—Up at 9. Got things ready for going to Diodati; settled accounts, etc. Left at 3; went to Diodati; went back to dinner, and then returned. Shelley etc. came to tea, and we sat talking till 11. My rooms are so:

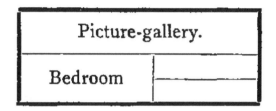

June 11.—Wrote home and to Pryse Gordon. Read Lucian. Went to Shelley's; dined; Shelley in the evening with us.

June 12.—Rode to town. Subscribed to a circulating library, and went in the evening to Madame Odier. Found no one. Miss O[dier], to make time pass, played the Ranz des Vaches— plaintive and war-like. People arrived. Had a confab with Dr. O. about perpanism,[9] etc. Began dancing: waltzes, cotillons, French country-dances and English ones: first time I shook my feet to French measure. Ladies all waltzed except the English: *they* looked on frowning. Introduced to Mrs. Slaney: invited me for next night. You ask without introduction; the girls refuse those they dislike. Till 12. Went and slept at the Balance.

June 13.—Rode home, and to town again. Went to Mrs. Slaney: a ball. Danced and played at chess. Walked home in thunder and lightning: lost my way. Went back in search of some one—fell upon the police. Slept at the Balance.

June 14.—Rode home—rode almost all day. Dined with Rossi, who came to us; shrewd, quick, manly-minded fellow; like him very much. Shelley etc. fell in in the evening.

June 15.—Up late; began my letters. Went to Shelley's. After dinner, jumping a wall my foot slipped and I strained my left ankle. Shelley etc. came in the evening; talked of my play etc., which all agreed was worth nothing. Afterwards Shelley and I had a conversation about principles,—whether man was to be thought merely an instrument.

[The accident to Polidori's ankle was related thus by Byron in a letter addressed from Ouchy to John Murray. "Dr. Polidori is not here, but at Diodati; left behind in hospital with a sprained ankle, acquired in tumbling from a wall—he can't jump." Thomas Moore, in his *Life of Byron*, supplies some details. "Mrs. Shelley was, after a shower of rain, walking up the hill to Diodati; when Byron, who saw her from his balcony where he was standing with Polidori, said to the latter: 'Now you who wish to be gallant ought to jump down this small height, and offer your arm.' Polidori tried to do so; but, the ground being wet, his foot slipped and he sprained his ankle. Byron helped to carry him in, and, after he was laid on the sofa, went up-stairs to fetch a pillow for him. 'Well, I did not believe you had so much feeling,' was Polidori's ungracious remark."

The play written by Polidori, which received so little commendation, was, I suppose, the *Cajetan* which is mentioned at an early point in the Journal. There was another named *Boadicea*, in prose; very poor stuff, and I suppose written at an early date. A different drama named *Ximenes* was afterwards published: certainly its merit—whether as a drama or as a specimen of poetic writing—is slender. The conversation between Shelley and Polidori about "principles"and "whether man was to be thought merely an instrument" appears to have some considerable analogy with a conversation to which Mary Shelley and Professor Dowden refer, and which raised in her mind a train of thought conducing to her invention of Frankenstein and his Man-monster. Mary, however, speaks of Byron (not Polidori) as the person who conversed with Shelley on that occasion.

Professor Dowden, paraphrasing some remarks made by Mary,
says: "One night she sat listening to a conversation between the
two poets at Diodati. What was the nature, they questioned, of
the principle of life? Would it ever be discovered, and the power
of communicating life be acquired? Perhaps a corpse would be
reanimated; galvanism had given token of such things. That
night Mary lay sleepless," etc.]

June 16.—Laid up. Shelley came, and dined and slept here, with
Mrs. S[helley] and Miss Clare Clairmont. Wrote another letter.

[This is the first instance in which the name of Miss Clairmont
is given correctly by Polidori; but it may be presumed that he
had, several days back, found out that she was not properly to be
termed "Miss Godwin."]

June 17.—Went into the town; dined with Shelley etc. here.
Went after dinner to a ball at Madame Odier's; where I was
introduced to Princess Something and Countess Potocka, Poles,
and had with them a long confab. Attempted to dance, but felt
such horrid pain was forced to stop. The ghost-stories are begun
by all but me.

[This date serves to rectify a small point in literary history.
We all know that the party at Cologny—consisting of Byron and
Polidori on the one hand, and of Shelley and Mrs. Shelley and
Miss Clairmont on the other—undertook to write each of them
an independent ghost-story, or story of the supernatural; the
result being Byron's fragment of *The Vampyre*, Polidori's complete
story of *The Vampyre*, and Mrs. Shelley's renowned *Frankenstein*.
Shelley and Miss Clairmont proved defaulters. It used to be said
that Matthew Gregory Lewis, author of *The Monk*, had been
mixed up in the same project; but this is a mistake, for Lewis
only reached the Villa Diodati towards the middle of August.
Professor Dowden states as follows: "During a few days of ungenial
weather which confined them to the house [by "them" Shelley
and the two ladies are evidently meant, and perhaps also Byron
and Polidori] some volumes of ghost-stories, *Fantasmagoriana,
ou Recueil d'Histoires d'Apparitions, de Spectres, Revenans*, etc.

89

(a collection translated into French from the German) fell into their hands, and its perusal probably excited and overstrained Shelley's imagination." Professor Dowden then proceeds to narrate an incident connected with Coleridge's *Christabel*, of which more anon; and he says that immediately *after* that incident Byron proposed, "We will each write a ghost-story"—a suggestion to which the others assented. It is only fair to observe that Professor Dowden's account corresponds with that which Polidori himself supplied in the proem to his tale of *The Vampyre*. But Polidori's Diary proves that this is not absolutely correct. The ghost-stories (prompted by the *Fantasmagoriana*, a poor sort of book) had already been begun by Byron, Shelley, Mrs. Shelley, and Miss Clairmont, not later than June 17, whereas the *Christabel* incident happened on June 18. Byron's story, as I have already said, was *The Vampyre*, left a fragment; Shelley's is stated to have been some tale founded on his own early experiences—nothing farther is known of it; Mrs. Shelley's was eventually *Frankenstein*, but, from the details which have been published as to the first conception of this work, we must assume that what she had begun by June 17 was something different: of Miss Clairmont's story no sort of record remains.

The Countess Potocka, whom Polidori mentions, was a lady belonging to the highest Polish nobility, grand-niece of Stanislaus Augustus Poniatowski, who had been King of Poland up to 1798. She was daughter of Count Tyszkiewicz, and married Count Potocki, and afterwards Count Wonsowicz. Born in 1776, she lived on to 1867, when she died in Paris, a leader of society under the Second Empire. Thus she was forty years old when Polidori saw her. She wrote memoirs of her life, going up to 1820: a rather entertaining book, dealing with many important transactions, especially of the period of Napoleon I: she gives one to understand that this supreme potentate was rather susceptible to her charms, but a rival compatriot, the Countess Walewska, was then in the ascendant. I have seen reproductions from two portraits of the Countess Potocka, both of them ascribed to Angelica Kauffman:

one of these shows a strikingly handsome young woman, with dark eyes of singular brilliancy and sentiment. Its date cannot be later than 1807, when the painter died, and may probably be as early as 1800.]

June 18.—My leg much worse. Shelley and party here. Mrs. S[helley] called me her brother (younger). Began my ghost-story[10] after tea. Twelve o'clock, really began to talk ghostly. L[ord] B[yron] repeated some verses of Coleridge's *Christabel*, of the witch's breast; when silence ensued, and Shelley, suddenly shrieking and putting his hands to his head, ran out of the room with a candle. Threw water in his face, and after gave him ether. He was looking at Mrs. S[helley], and suddenly thought of a woman he had heard of who had eyes instead of nipples, which, taking hold of his mind, horrified him.—He married; and, a friend of his liking his wife, he tried all he could to induce her to love him in turn. He is surrounded by friends who feed upon him, and draw upon him as their banker. Once, having hired a house, a man wanted to make him pay more, and came trying to bully him, and at last challenged him. Shelley refused, and was knocked down; coolly said that would not gain him his object, and was knocked down again.—Slaney called.

[Some of these statements are passing strange, and most of them call for a little comment. First we hear that Mrs. Shelley called Polidori her younger brother—a designation which may have been endearing but was not accurate; for, whereas the doctor was aged 20 at this date, Mrs. Shelley was aged only 18. Next, Polidori, after tea, began his ghost-story. This, according to Mrs. Shelley, was a tale about "a skull-headed lady, who was so punished for peeping through a keyhole—what to see, I forget; something very shocking and wrong, of course." So says Mrs. Shelley: but Polidori's own statement is that the tale which he at first began was the one published under the title of *Ernestus Berchtold*, which contains nothing about a skull-headed lady: some details are given in my Introduction. Afterwards he took up the notion of a vampyre, when relinquished by Byron. The original story, *Ernestus Berchtold*, may possibly have been completed in 1816: at any rate it was completed at some time, and published in 1819, soon after *The Vampyre*. Then comes the incident (first published in my edition of Shelley's poems in 1870) of Byron repeating some lines from *Christabel*, and Shelley, who mixed them up with some fantastic idea already present to his mind, decamping with a shriek. The lines from *Christabel* are these—

> "Then drawing in her breath aloud,
> Like one that shuddered, she unbound
> The cincture from beneath her breast:
> Her silken robe and inner vest
> Dropped to her feet, and full in view
> Behold! her bosom and half her side,
> Hideous, deformed, and pale of hue—
> A sight to dream of, not to tell!
> And she is to sleep by Christabel!"

From this incident Polidori proceeds to three statements regarding occurrences in Shelley's life; it may be presumed that he had heard them from the poet in the course of this same evening. "A friend of his liking his wife, he tried all he could to induce her to love him in turn." Nothing of this sort appears in the authenticated facts of Shelley's life. It is certain that, very soon after he had married Harriet Westbrook in 1811, he saw reason for thinking that his friend Hogg "liked his wife," both of them being then in York; but, so far from "trying all he could to induce her to love him in turn," he at once took her away from York to Keswick, and he addressed letters of grave remonstrance and sad reproach to Hogg, and then for a time broke off all intercourse with him. The only other matter one knows of at all relevant to this issue is that Shelley alleged that afterwards a certain Major Ryan carried on an intrigue with Harriet. He blamed and resented her imputed frailty, and put it forward as a principal motive for his separating from her. It is certainly possible that, after the separation, he told Harriet that she might as well "make the best of a bad job," and adhere to Ryan, since she would not adhere to her wedded husband: but no indication of any such advice on his part appears anywhere else. Be it understood that I do not at all affirm that this suspicion or statement of Shelley's about Harriet and Ryan was correct. I doubt it extremely, though not venturing summarily to reject it. The next point is that Shelley was "surrounded by friends who feed upon him, and draw upon him as their banker." This probably glances at Godwin, and perhaps also at Charles Clairmont, the brother of Clare. Thomas Love Peacock may likewise be in question: not Leigh Hunt, for, though the cap might have fitted him in and after the year 1817, it did not so in the present year 1816, since Hunt was as yet all but unknown to our poet. Last comes the funny statement about a hectoring landlord who twice knocked down the non-duelling author of *Queen Mab*. It is difficult to guess what this allegation may refer to. Shelley had by this time had several landlords in different parts of the United Kingdom; and quite possibly some of them thought his rent unduly low, or more especially his quarterly or other instalments irregularly paid, but who can have been the landlord who took the law so decisively into his own hands, and found so meekly unresisting a tenant, I have no idea. There was an odd incident on January 19, 1812, when Shelley, then living at Keswick, was (or was said to have been) struck down senseless on the threshold of his door—seemingly by a couple of robbers. On that occasion, however, his landlord, Mr. Dare, appeared in the character of a guardian angel: so we must dismiss any notion that this incident, the one which in some of its features seems to come nearest the mark, is that which Shelley so ingenuously imparted to Polidori.]

June 19.—Leg worse; began my ghost-story. Mr. S[helley?] etc. forth here. Bonstetten and Rossi called. B[onstetten] told me a story of the religious feuds in Appenzel; a civil war between Catholics and Protestants. Battle arranged; chief advances; calls the other. Calls himself and other fools, for battles will not

THE DIARY OF
DR. JOHN WILLIAM POLIDORI

persuade of his being wrong. Other agreed, and persuaded them to take the boundary rivulet; they did. Bed at 3 as usual.

June 20.—My leg kept me at home. Shelley etc. here.

June 21.—Same.

June 22.—L[ord] B[yron] and Shelley went to Vevay; Mrs. S[helley] and Miss Clare Clairmont to town. Went to Rossi's—had tired his patience. Called on Odier; Miss reading Byron.

[The expedition of Byron and Shelley to Vevay was that same Lake-voyage which forms so prominent an incident in their Swiss experiences. Their starting upon this expedition had hitherto been dated June 23. Professor Dowden has expressed a doubt whether June 22 would not be the correct date, and here we find that so it is.]

June 23.—Went to town; apologized to Rossi. Called on Dr. Slaney etc. Walked to Mrs. Shelley. Pictet, Odier, Slaney, dined with me. Went down to Mrs. S[helley?] for the evening. Odier mentioned the cases of two gentlemen who, on taking the nitrate of silver, some time after had a blacker face. Pictet confirmed it.

June 24.—Up at 12. Dined down with Mrs. S[helley] and Miss C[lare] C[lairmont].

[The dates hereabouts become somewhat embarrassing. For the day which I am calling June 24 Polidori repeats June 23; and he continues with the like sequence of days up to June 29, when, as he notes, he "found Lord Byron and Shelley returned." It seems to be an established fact that the day when Shelley got back to Montalègre was July 1: he has stated so, and a note to the *Letters of Lord Byron* states the same. Thus Polidori seems to have dropped two days. One is accounted for by substituting June 24 for June 23; and I shall call the next day June 26, though uncertain as to where the second error occurs.]

June 26.—Up. Mounted on horseback: went to town. Saw Mrs. Shelley: dined. To Dr. Rossi's party of physicians: after at Mrs. S[helley's?].

June 27.—Up at Mrs. Shelley's: dined. No calèche arrived: walked to G[eneva]. No horses: ordered saddle-horse. Walked to

Rossi's—gone. Went to the gate: found him. Obliged to break off theappointment. Went to Odier's. Met with Mr. ——, a friend of Lord Byron's father. Invited me to his house: been a long time on the Continent. Music, ranz des vaches, beautiful. Rode two hours; went to Mrs. S[helley]; Miss C[lairmont] talked of a soliloquy.

[This last phrase is not clear: does it mean that Miss Clairmont talked *in* a soliloquy—talked to herself, in such a way as to excite observation?]

June 28.—All day at Mrs. S[helley's].

June 29.—Up at 1; studied; down at Mrs. S[helley's].

June 30.—Same.

July 1.—Went in calèche to town with Mrs. S[helley] and C[lare] for a ride, and to mass (which we did not go to, being begun). Dined at 1. Went to town to Rossi. Introduced to Marchese Saporati; together to Mr. Saladin of Vaugeron, Countess Breuss, Calpnafur; and then to a party of ladies.

[The word which I give as Calpnafur is dubious in Charlotte Polidori's transcript: it is evidently one of those words as to which she felt uncertain, and she wrote it as near to Dr. Polidori's script as she could manage. The other three names—Saporati, Saladin, and Breuss—are not elucidated in any book I have consulted. Perhaps Saporati ought to be Saporiti—see p. 149. There were two Saladins of some note in France in the days of the Revolution and Empire—one of them lived on to 1832; but I can scarcely think that this Saladin in Geneva was of the same race. He may be the "Syndic Saladin" mentioned farther on.]

Found Lord Byron and Shelley returned.

July 2.—Rain all day. In the evening to Mrs. S[helley].

September 5.—Not written my Journal till now through neglect and dissipation. Had a long explanation with S[helley] and L[ord] B[yron] about my conduct to L[ord] B[yron]; threatened to shoot S[helley] one day on the water. Horses been a subject of quarrel twice, Berger having accused me of laming one.

[Before this date, September 5, Shelley, with Mary and Miss

Clairmont, had finally left the neighbourhood of Geneva; they started on August 29 upon their return journey to England. The statement that Polidori "threatened to shoot Shelley one day on the water" brings us back again to that question, of which I spoke under the date of June 4, about some hare-brained quarrel with Shelley leading to a challenge for a duel. The natural inference from the position which this entry occupies in Polidori's Diary certainly is that the threat to Shelley occurred at some date between July 2 and August 28—not at the earlier date of June 4; and so I presume it more probably did. We find also that Polidori's conduct in relation to Byron was considered not to be correct; and this formed the subject of "a long explanation" not only with Byron himself but likewise with Shelley.]

L[ord] B[yron] went to town in pursuit of thieves who came to steal the anchors after having stolen my sail. Was refused permission to go out. I went to the Syndic Saladin, and told him I begged his pardon for our servants, who must have said something insulting, or else he could not have refused permission to leave the port. Thieves attempted to break into the house.

An apothecary sold some bad magnesia to L[ord] B[yron]. Found it bad by experiment of sulphuric acid colouring it red rose-colour. Servants spoke about it. Appointed Castan to see experiment; came; impudent; refused to go out; collared him, sent him out, broke spectacles. Laid himself on a wall for three hours; refused to see experiments. Saw L[ord] B[yron], told him his tale before two physicians. Brought me to trial before five judges; had an advocate to plead. I pleaded for myself; laughed at the advocate. Lost his cause on the plea of calumny; made me pay 12 florins for the broken spectacles and costs. Magnesia chiefly alumina, as proved by succenate[11] and carbonate of ammonia.

Dined twice at Madame de Staël's; visited there also; met Madame de Broglie and M[onsieur?]; Miss Randall; two Roccas; Schlegel; Monsignor Brema; Dumont; Bonstetten; Madame Bottini; Madame Mongelas; young de Staël.

[It will be observed that Dr. Polidori, although he details these

various circumstances likely to create some soreness between
Lord Byron and himself, does not here state in express terms
that the poet had parted with him. At the end of this entry for
September 5 he does, however, give a few words to the subject,
confirmatory of Lord Byron's ensuing remarks. Byron, in a good-
humoured spirit, gave a general explanation in a letter addressed
to John Murray on January 24, 1817. He understood that Polidori
was "about to return to England, to go to the Brazils on a medical
speculation with the Danish Consul" (which, however, he did
not actually do); and Byron asked Murray to get the Doctor any
letters of recommendation. Then he adds: "He understands his
profession well, and has no want of general talent: his faults are
the faults of a pardonable vanity and youth. His remaining with
me was out of the question. I have enough to do to manage my
own scrapes; and, as precepts without example are not the most
gracious homilies, I thought it better to give him his *congé*: but
I know no great harm of him, and some good. He is clever and
accomplished; knows his profession, by all accounts, well; and is
honourable in his dealings, and not at all malevolent." In March
1820 Byron made a few other observations applicable to his
intercourse with Polidori: "The sole companion of my journey
was a young physician who had to make his way in the world,
and, having seen very little of it, was naturally and laudably
desirous of seeing more society than suited my present habits or
my past experience. I therefore presented him to those gentlemen
of Geneva for whom I had letters of introduction; and, having
thus seen him in a situation to make his own way, retired for my
own part entirely from society, with the exception of one English
family"—*i.e.* Shelley and his two ladies. At times, however,
Byron was less lenient to the Doctor. On June 17, 1817, he wrote
to Murray: "I never was much more disgusted with any human
production than with the eternal nonsense and *tracasseries* and
emptiness and ill-humour and vanity of that young person: but
he has some talent, and is a man of honour, and has dispositions
of amendment in which he has been aided by a little subsequent

experience, and may turn out well."

It may be hardly needful to state that "Madame de Broglie and Monsieur" (*i.e.* the Duc Victor de Broglie) were the daughter and son-in-law of Madame de Staël: they were now but very recently wedded, February 20, 1816. Byron thought the youthful wife devoted to her husband, and said "Nothing was more pleasing than to see the development of the domestic affections in a very young woman." Of the two Roccas, one is remembered as Madame de Staël's second husband. He was a very handsome officer of Swiss origin. They married privately in 1811, she being then aged about forty-five, and he twenty-two. He only survived his wife about six months, dying in 1818. August Wilhelm von Schlegel was at this date about forty-nine years old, celebrated as a translator of Shakespear and Calderon, and as a scholar of extensive range. He had travelled much with Madame de Staël, who drew on him for some of the ideas set forth in her book *De l'Allemagne.* Monsignor Brema is a good deal mentioned farther on: he was a son of the Marchese di Brema (or Brême), who had been a valuable Minister of the Interior under the Napoleonic *régime* in Italy. Dumont, who has been previously named by Polidori as the translator of Bentham, was also closely associated with the great Mirabeau.]

At Vaugeron, the Saladins, Auguste Mathould, Rossi, Jacques Naple [?], Brelaz, Clemann, Countess Mouskinpouskin, Breuss, Abate Gatelier, Toffettheim e figlio, Foncet, Saussure, Lord Breadalbane and family, a ball; Saladin of Maligny, Slaneys, two balls; Dr. and Mrs. Freckton White, Galstons (Miss etc. sisters), a ball; Lord Bingham, Lord F. Cunningham, Lord Belgray, a ball; Mr. Tillotson St. Aubyn, Mrs. Trevanion, Valence Meers, R. Simmons, Lloyd, Princess Jablonski, Lady Hamilton Dalrymple, Odiers, Lord Kinnoul, Somers, Lord Glenorchy, Mr. Evans, Coda (songstress), M. G. Lewis, Mrs. Davies, Mr. Pictet, Mr. Hobhouse, Dr. Gardner, Caravella, Shelleys, Sir John St. Aubyn.

[Most of these numerous names must be left to themselves: several of them are hereafter commented, often caustically, by

Polidori himself. Saussure is not the more celebrated naturalist and traveller, Horace Benedict, who died in 1799; but is his son, Nicolas Théodore, who coöperated largely with the father, and produced an important book of his own, *Recherches sur la Végétation*. Born in 1767, he lived on to 1845. Mrs. Trevanion may be supposed to have belonged to the same family as a certain Mr. Trevanion who figured very discreditably in the history of that Medora Leigh who was the daughter of the Honourable Mrs. Leigh (Byron's half sister) and ostensibly of her husband, but who is now said to have been in fact the daughter of Byron himself. Lady Hamilton Dalrymple ought seemingly to be Lady Dalrymple Hamilton: she was a daughter of Viscount Duncan, and wife of Sir Hew D. Hamilton. Somers is mentioned on p. 150: this is probably the correct spelling, not (as here) Summers. Matthew Gregory Lewis (whom I had occasion to name before) was the author of *The Monk*, which he wrote at the early age of nineteen, of the musical drama *The Castle Spectre*, and of other works whose celebrity has not survived into the present day. He was now near the end of his brief career, for he died in 1818, aged forty-two.]

The society I have been in may be divided into three sets: the canton of Genthoud, Coppet, and Geneva. The canton is an assemblage of a neighbourhood of about seven or eight families, meeting alternately on Sundays at each other's houses, and every Thursday at the Countess Breuss's. The Countess Breuss lives at Genthoud in a villa she has bought. She has two husbands, one in Russia, one at Venice; she acted plays at the Hermitage under Catherine. Not being able to get a divorce, she left Russia, went to Venice for six days, stayed as many years, married (it is said), bought villas etc. in the Venetian's name, and separated. Her family consists of Madame Gatelier, a humble friend, a great lover of medicaments etc., Abate —— ——, her Almoner, an excellent Brescian, great lover of religionists. A mania in the family for building summer-houses, porticoes, and baths; neatly planned; an island with a ditch round it; a Tower of Babel round the trunk of a chestnut; a summer-house by the roadside of a Moorish construction. The Countess is very good-natured, laughs where others calumniate and talk scandal with prudish airs, kind to all. The society is extremely pleasant; generally dancing or music. It was the birthday of Charles Saladin, who, having been four years in Nap[oleon]'s army, knew nothing of the matter. She asked to have the fêting of him. They acted first a charade on the canton of Genthoud. She acted with Mr. Massey junior, with others, and myself as a woman—the words to blind.[12] Then came a kind of farce, in which Charles was dressed as the C. B. [Countess Breuss?], Gatelier as the Abbé, and Miss Saladin as Gatelier: each took one another off. Written by C. B. When at last another of the society brought a letter announcing it to be Charles' birthday. Then they, while he was in his amazement, sang a song to him, presented him with a bouquet and purse. Then an elegant supper, and afterwards a ball on the arrival of Madame Toffettheim with her son. A great party was invited; and after tea two plays were acted—*Le Pachà de Suresne* and *Les Ricochets*. There was an immense number of spectators. The actors were, in *Le Pachà de Suresne*, Madame Dorsan, la Comtesse Breuss; Laure, Madlle. Brelaz; Aglaé, Clemann; Nathalie, M.; Madlle. Remy, Madame Gatelier; Perceval, Alexis Saladin; Flicflac, Polidori; Joseph, C. Saladin.—*Les Ricochets*—I do not remember the characters. The actors were Alexis, Charles, Auguste Saladin, Massey le jeune, La Comtesse Breuss, Madame Mathilde Saladin. The rehearsals before were frequent.

I got a discretion from the Countess, which I took in the shape of a Swiss,[13] in consequence of a wager that I could not go straight home.

La Toffettheim is a nice, unpretending, lady-like woman, pleasing and affectionate. Her son full of liberty-ideas. It was here, in consequence of Massey junior dancing extremely well, that, being defied, I danced a pantaloon-dance, by which I made enemies; for, upon my refusing it at the Saladins', they thought it was a personal refusal. Saladins of Vaugeron, father and mother.

Father deaf, good-natured: said to me upon reading my thesis, "Mais, Monsieur, il n'y a pas de paradoxe." The mother pretended to play shy on account of Madame B.

[By Madame B. it would appear, from a statement farther on, that Polidori means Madame Brelaz.]

The daughter—because, the first night I saw her, knowing her by particular introduction, I stuck to her—thought me in love, and said so,—fool! Madame Mathilde [Saladin] pretended prude in mine and Madame B.'s case, while she herself has got Mr. Massey junior dangling, not unheard, after her. Charles a good boisterous soldier, at Leipzig, Nassau, and 13 ingwen [?] [14] Waterloo business. Makes up for wit by noise, for affection by slaps on the back. On his birthday I addressed him with (after supper)—

"Jeune guerrier dans l'armée du premier des héros,
Dans la cause de la France dédaignant le repos,
Que la chute de vos ans soit tranquille et heureuse,
Comme fut l'aube de vos jours éclatante et glorieuse."

[This little specimen suffices to show that Polidori had no true idea of French versification: he was evidently unaware that a final *e* mute coming before a consonant counts as a syllable.]

Auguste, a simple neat fool, despising learning because he is noble and has enough to live upon; content to dangle, with a compliment and a sentiment, after a woman's tail. Alexis, so so, good-naturedly ignorant husband to Mathilde. Massey senior, active pleasant man, excellent fencer and dancer—been secretary to Bertrand. Massey junior, confident, impudent, insolent, ignorant puppy. Saladins of Maligny, neither good nor bad, rich: to gain a little more, let their villa to Lord Breadalbane, and retired to a cottage, though both old and only one ugly vain daughter. Lord Breadalbane, an excellent, good-sensed though not quick man: answered—when the Duke of Bedford said to him, "What would you give to have the Breadalbane estate in

Bedfordshire?"—"Why, your Grace, I should be sorry if my estate
would go in Bedfordshire." Gave a very good ball at which I was.
His son Lord Glenorchy, good, shy, not brilliant young man.
His lady not spoken to. His daughter excellent dancer, rather
haughty. Mr. Evans, a good sensible man, biassed in his thoughts
by his cassock. At the society he took up the immortality: Lord
Glenorchy gave a positive No. Saussure, Mrs., a wax talkative
figure. Mr., a would-be scientific gentleman: thought me a fool
because I danced pantaloon, and himself a wise man because he
knows the names of his father's stones. Jacquet, Madlle., got half
in love with her,—no, her 8000 a year: her face and bad-singing
exposures cured me. Foncet, officer of the Piedmontese troops,
jealous of him.

Brelaz, Portuguese lady,—in love with her; I think fond of me
too; imprudent; her daughter also against me on account of it;
shows it too much publicly; very jealous; her daughters, sprightly
good-looking girls. Clemann—got half in love with her; nice
daughter. The Cavalier pleasing. Had a dispute in a public ball
with her two fools. One of the Saladins, Auguste, courts her,
and she laughs; she excites love in every young man's breast.
Miss Harriet is rather too serious for her age, pretty and well-
informed in novels and romances, and rather too sentimental.
Cavalier's Marianne is a fine hoydenish creature: applies when
studying, and romps when playing.

Madame de Staël I have dined with three times; she is better,
those who know her say, at home than abroad. She has married
poor Rocca. She talks much; would not believe me to be a
physician; presented her my thesis, which she told me she had
read with pleasure. Talked about religion, and puts down every
[?] of Rocca. Ugly; good eyes. Writing on the French Revolution;
polite, affable; lectures, and tells all to L[ord] B[yron]. Madame
de Broglie, her daughter, a beautiful, dirty-skinned woman;
pleasant, soft-eyed speaker; dances well, waltzes. Schlegel, a
presumptuous literato, contradicting *à outrance*; a believer in
magnetism. Rocca, a talkative, good-natured, beautiful man, with

a desire for knowledge; the author of *Walcheren* and *Espagne*; excellent at naïve description. Rocca, the judge, very clever and quick, rising; know little of him. Been seven years in the courtship of Miss Saladin; she neither refuses nor accepts him, but keeps him in her train. Miss Randall, sister to Mrs. Norgate. Monsignor Brema, friend of Ugo Foscolo, enthusiastic for Italy, encomiast in all, Grand Almoner of Italy, hater of Austrians. Dumont, a thick, heavy-thoughted body, editor of Bentham. Bonstetten, friend of Gray.

The first time L[ord] B[yron] went, there was Mrs. Hervey there; talkative, sister and a great friend of the Noels; she thought proper to faint out of the house, though her curiosity brought her back to speak with him.

Bonstetten told me that, upon his saying to Gray that he must be happy, he took and read to him the criticism of Johnson, which happens to have been written after Gray's death; he used to go in the evening to tea, and remain all night reading the English authors with him. Gray introduced him to society;[15] and, one of the professors having asked him if he understood what he said, he replied he thought so, but very diff[idently?]—"So you think so only!" Gray, hearing this, showed B[onstetten] some passages to ask *him*, which B[onstetten] did in a public company, complimenting him upon [his?] known knowledge; when all the company, one after the other, began contradicting the Professor's opinion. Then B[onstetten], turning to him, said, "You perhaps thought *you* understood Shakespear." Gray told him that there was none who could *perfectly* understand him.

Rossi, an Italian of about thirty, pleasant, agreeable, and good-natured, professor at Bologna, thence obliged to fly with two others. One of his companions was beginning his lecture, when the students called out, "No lecture, but an improvise upon the liberty of Italy"; as he was an improvisatore. He objected, as, on account of Murat's approach, it might be suspicious. They insisted, and the professors at hand said, "No harm if not upon present circumstances." He did it, and the students issued forth to join Murat; they had however made up their minds to do so before. Rossi joined it more openly and loudly, and was obliged to fly. He wrote a memoir to defend himself, in which he said it was only to avoid the Roman dominion, and give it to the Archduke; who told him that he had better write another, as Bologna was already ceded to Pius. When he was ruined thus partially he wrote to the father of his betrothed, to say that he must not (if he chose) think himself bound by his promise, as he was not in the same circumstances as when the promise was given. The father did retract. So far a man of honour. Now how to reconcile his being with Calandion, a magistrate of G[eneva] violent on the other side? who says he has made a good profession to him, and at the same time professing other opinions to others.

Gave me a letter to Milan, and by him I have been introduced to Saporiti, a good, enthusiastic, ignorant Italian. Talked of the English landing 100,000 soldiers here and there, as if they were so many peas.

Slaneys: the husband jealous of every one—Cambridge degree. When I danced with his wife, he after, when walking with her, came up and gave an arm too. The wife beautiful, but very simple. Galston, Miss, very beautiful.

"Genevan Liberal Society" is a muster of Englishmen for debate on speculative questions. Twice there. Immortality, accomplice's evidence. The members whom I knew were—Lord Kinnoul, a most tiresome, long-winded, repeating, thick-headed would-be orator, Lord Conyngham.

[The MS. gives "Cunningham," which must be a mistake. The Lord Conyngham of this period began the year 1816 as an Earl, and ended it as a Marquis. He was born in 1766, and lived on to 1832, and was husband of a lady, Elizabeth Denison, whose name figures much in the gossip, not excluding the scandal, of those years.]

Mr. Somers, good head enough. Valence, whom I cried to hear; and, meeting me after at Chamounix, the first thing he asked me was, "Why did you laugh at me?" St. Aubyn, Lloyd, Slaney.

Lloyd, of good Welsh blood, his original name Ap Griffith, rode out. We went out visiting one day, and, in returning in his gig, he touched a horse of a row of carts. The carter struck me upon my back with his whip; I jumped down, and six jumped at me. I fortunately was between a wheel and a hedge, so that they all could not reach. Lloyd, seeing this, jumped down also; then three left me and went to him, and another untied a piece of his wagon with which, while I defended myself from the two (one with a whip), he struck me while fortunately my arm was striking a blow, so that it did but just touch my face. He lifted again; I sprang back, and with all the force of my leap struck him with my fist in his face. His blow fell to the ground, and with his hand to his nose he retreated. They then seized stones to throw, but we closed with them; they could not throw above two, when we saw an English carriage we knew coming. We called, they came, and immediately the boisterous [fellows?] were calm. Some who tried to divide us got blows also.

St. Aubyn, an excellent fellow, introduced me to his father at Genthoud: is a natural son, studying for the Church. His father is a good polite man, according to the "go" school.[16] Keeps a mistress now, though sixty-five years: has many children by different mistresses.

At Dr. Odier's—who is a good old, toothless, chatty, easy-believing man—there was a society every Wednesday, where I went sometimes. They danced, sang, ate cakes, and drank tea; English almost entirely, changing every Wednesday.—Went to a concert of Madamigella Coda—the theatre dirty.

When Mr. Hobhouse and Davies arrived, we went to Chamounix. The first day through Chesne, Annemasse, Vetra, Nangy, Contamine, Bonneville (dinner), Cluses, Sallenches (slept). Next day by Chede in two *char-à-bancs*, with each a guide; a fine pine-glen of the Arve, to Chamounix. We went that evening over the Brisson, and to the source of the Aveyron. Next day so bad we left, and returned to Sallenches, taking the fall of Chede in our way; thence to Diodati. Mr. Scrope Davies played against the marker at tennis: then went, taking Rushton with him. [Rushton was one of the servants.]

L[ord] B[yron] determined upon our parting,—not upon any quarrel, but on account of our not suiting. Gave me £70; 50 for 3 months and 20 for voyage. Paid away a great deal, and then thought of setting off: determined for Italy. Madame de Staël gave me three letters. Madame B[relaz?] wept, and most seemed sorry.

[I suppose that most likely the "Madame B." here is Madame Brelaz, with whom, as stated on p. 145, Polidori was "in love." Or it might perhaps be the Comtesse de Breuss.]

The night before I went, at Madame B[reuss?]'s, they acted *C'est le Même* extremely well; a Lausanne girl acting the lady very well. The costumes also extremely good. Wished nobody good-bye: told them, though, I was going. Set off with 47 louis, 112 naps.

Le Valais from Schürer's book, *Description du Département du Simplon*, 1812, lent me by the Cav[aliere]. See elsewhere.

September 16.—Left Cologny and Lord Byron at six in the morning. Breakfasted at Doraine, 3 leagues. Dined, Thouson, ditto. Evrein, 2. Slept St. Gingoux, 4. Passed Meillerie. Saw Lausanne at a distance, right through this part of Sardinian King's dominions. Read Madame Brelaz's verses. Wept—not at them, but at the prose.

September 17.—Left St. Gingoux at 6. Walked to ——.[17] Took bread and wine. Crossed to Chillon. Saw Bonivard's prison for six years; whence a Frenchman had broken, and, passing through a window, swam to a boat. Instruments of torture,—the pulley. Three soldiers there now: the Roman arms already affixed. Large subterranean passes. Saw in passing the three treed islands. The Rhone enters by two mouths, and keeps its waters distinct for two stones' throw.

From Chillon I went to Montreaux—breakfasted—leaving Charney on my left. I began to mount towards the Dent de Jamanu. Before beginning to mount Jamanu itself, one has a beautiful view, seeing only part of the lake, bound by Meillerie, Roches, and the Rhone. Higher up the view is more extensive, but not so beautiful—nothing being distinct; the water looking merely as an inlet of sky, but one could see the Jura as far as Genthoud.

I entered a chalet, where they expressed great astonishment at my drinking whey, which they give to their pigs only. Refused at first money.

Descended towards Mont Boyon. What owing to the fatigue and hardly meeting any one, sick with grief. At Mont Boyon dined, and, finding they would not dance, slept immediately after.

September 18.—Up at 4. Drank wine and bread. At 6 set off. Passed the Château d'Ox where there was a fair. After that, hardly met a soul. Always on the side of the mountains, each side of a river or torrent; with torrent-beds, pine-forests, chalets, villages without a visible soul—all at work—and ups and downs: so that this road, if I had not had that of yesterday, I should have called the worst in the world. Passed through Château d'Ox; Rougemont, breakfast; Zwezermann, dinner; Gessenay; Lambeck; Reichenstein; Weissenbach; Bottingen, tea and night. The French language leaves off at Gessenay (rather, patois), and they begin their German: found it difficult to go on.

September 19.—Got up at 4-1/2. Set off from Bottingen. Went through Obernoyle. Breakfasted at Wyssenbach: refused my money. Went to the Doctor, who charged me a nap. Went through Erlenbach, Lauterbach, Meiningen, to Thun. Splendid scenery; especially the first look at the Lake by the river's mouth, and the pass into a great valley. Took dinner, and then a warm bath. Arrived at 1 o'clock. All the houses are of wood, the foundation only being stone: great cut ornaments between the rows of windows: the wood, fir. Felt very miserable, especially these two last days: only met two persons to whom I could speak—the others all Germans. At Wyssenbach they all said grace before breakfast, and then ate out of the same dish; remarking (as I understood them) that I, not being a Catholic, would laugh.

[It was a mistake to suppose that Dr. Polidori was "not a Catholic." He was brought up as a Catholic, and never changed his religion, but may (I suppose) have been something of a sceptic.]

September 20.—Got up at 6. Wrote to St. Aubyn, Brelaz, father, Vaccà, and Zio, asking letters; to my father, to announce my parting.

[Vaccà was a celebrated surgeon at Pisa, of whom we shall hear farther. Zio is "my uncle"—*i.e.* Luigi Polidori, also at Pisa.]

Bought fresh shoes and stockings; found no book-seller's shop. The man at the post-office made a good reflection: that he was astonished so many came to see what they who were so near never want to see, and that he supposed that the English also leave much unseen in their own country.

Thun is a neat well-situated town, not large, with arcades—as apparently all the Berne towns. Afraid all day my dog was poisoned; which grieved me so, at seeing it vomit, that I wept. At 2 o'clock went in search of a boat: none going immediately, I walked along the left bank of the lake to Unterseen. The views the most beautiful I ever saw; through pines over precipices, torrents, and sleepers [?][18] and the best-cultivated fields I ever saw. The lake sometimes some hundred precipitous feet below my feet; at other times quite close to its edge; boats coming from the fair; picturesque towered villages; fine Alps on the other side, the Jungfrau and others far off. The bottom of the lake is especially magnificent. Lost my way, and had two little children as guides back again. One small cascade of seven or eight fountains.

Arrived at 7 at Unterseen: through Nilterfingen, Oberhofen, Rottingen, Morlangen, Neuchaus, to Unterseen. Found two Englishmen at supper: sat down with them. Very miserable all the morning.

September 21.—Got up at 6, having determined to go with the two to the Grindenwald in a *char-à-banc*, on account of the state of my foot. I went to the bridge at Interlachen to see the view coming between two beautiful isolated crags. Going, met a man, a maréchal, who had been to Vienna and Bohemia *en roulant* after his apprenticeship, to see the world—stopping a day at one place, a day at another. Returned, breakfasted: and then, after growling at the innkeeper's wishing us to take two horses, we went off through splendid pine-clad craggy valleys through Zweihitschirne to Lauterbrunner; whence to the fall of the Staubach, a bare cataract of 900 feet high, becoming vapour before it arrives—appearing much, and ending in a little stream. The curate of this village receives guests: there were the Prince Saxe-Gotha and family. We lunched at the inn, and went back to Lauterbrunner after having looked at the Jungfrau at a distance.

Went from Zweihitschirne to the Grindenwald with the Saxe-Gotha before us, through a more beautiful valley. Saw the glaciers come into it, with the Eiger, Wetterhorn, and other mountains, most magnificent. Walking about, found two girls who gave us cherries and chatted freely. Found that mules were 18 francs a day. A party came in in the dark at 8 with guides, hallooing and making a lively sound. Dined at 7, and talked about mules, hoping to get return ones etc.

September 22.—Got up. Could not get mules under 18 francs: my foot too bad to walk. Went with Captain Rice and others back to Interlachen. Got into a boat rowed by two men and a boy. Went by Brientz, Calne, to the Griesbach cascade, and then to Brientz—wilder, but not so beautiful as the Lake of Thun. The cascade I did not mount to see on account of my foot. At Brientz an old woman would give us her presence and conversation till one of my companions courted the daughter. Met between Grindenwald and Interlachen L[ord] B[yron] and Mr. H[obhouse]: we saluted.

September 23.—Got up at 4. Tired of my company; and, finding the expense more than I could afford, I went to their bedrooms to wish them good-bye. Set off at 5-1/2; and through fine copse-wooded crags, along the Aar, with cascades on every side, to Meyringen; where I breakfasted with two Germans, an old and a young artist—the old, chatty. Bought a pole. Went to see the Reichenbach, a fine cascade indeed. Thence through the beautiful vale of Nach-im-Grunden, where for a moment I planned a sovereignty; but, walking on, my plans faded before I arrived at Guttannen, where I dined.

Rode all the way to-day—horrible, only passable for men and mules: it is the way to St. Gothard. The road is merely huge unequal masses of granite thrown in a line not the straightest. From Guttannen the road went through the wildest and most sublime scenery I ever read of: vegetation less and less, so that, instead of grass, there was moss; then nothing. Instead of trees, shrubs; then nothing—huge granite rocks leaving hardly room for the road and river. The river's bed the most magnificent imaginable, cut deep and narrow into the solid rock, sinuous, and continually accompanied by cascades, and amazing bold and high single-arched bridges. Snow covering in some parts the whole bed of the river, and so thick and strong that even huge stones have fallen without injuring its crust. There are only two houses between Guttannen and the Hospital: one, a chalet wherein I entered; the other, a cow-herd's. Arrived at 6 o'clock precisely, having walked in only 9-1/2 hours 30 miles at least.

[This is a little indistinct in connexion with what precedes. I suppose that the phrase "rode all the way to-day" must be understood as meaning "all the way up to Guttannen"; and that, after leaving Guttannen, there were 30 miles of walking before the Hospital was reached. Yet this seems an unreasonably heavy day's work in travelling. After "only 9-1/2" the initial written is "m": but I presume it ought to be "h" (hours).]

The Hospital is an old stone ugly building, consonant with the wild scene, where the poor are lodged for nothing; others, us, [as?] an inn.

September 24.—On account of rain did not get up till 7. Set off across the Grimsel, a dreary mountain with snow in every hollow—5000 feet above the Four-canton Lake. Descended on the other side to Obergustellen, where I breakfasted at 10. Thence through Verlican, Guesquerman, Munster, Rexingen, Biel, Blizzen; where, out of the dead flat valley, I began to mount, and the scenery began to increase in beauty. One bridge especially over the Rhone, which fell between two clefts' sides, was beautiful. Sinderwald, Viesch, pine-wood; sax (?) along the rocks, and fine path along the mountain. Very fine, though continued hard rain, which drenched me and hindered my seeing a great deal. To Morel, where I went to bed, and ate a kind of dinner in bed at 7 o'clock.

September 25.—Up at 5; my foot, from having been obliged to walk with the shoe down at heel, very much swelled and too painful to walk. Breakfast. Two students from Brieg, of the Jesuits' College, came in, who had during the vacations been beyond Constance with only two *écus neufs* in their pockets. It costs them ten batches a year at College. Impudent one: the other modest-looking, but, when I gave him six francs because he had no more money, he asked me for more on other accounts. The Jesuits been restored two years.

At Brieg[19] I sent for the curate, a good old man of sixty. We conversed together in Latin for two hours; not at all troublesome in enquiries, but kind in answering them. The Valaisians resisted two years against the French in 93. It was the only part of the country in which they did so, except Unterwalden, and then it was only the peasants, and in every village there was a French party. The cruelty of the French was dreadful; they stuck their prisoners in a variety of ways like sheep. One old man of eighty, who had never left his house but whom they found eating, they strangled, and then put meat and bottles by him as if he had died apoplectic. They fought very hard and bravely, but such was the power of numbers united to the force of treachery that they were obliged to yield. In 1813, after the French had quitted Brieg, they again attempted to penetrate from Italy by the Simplon; when the Brieg, Kelor [?], and other villagers, joined by only one company of Austrians, surrounded them in the night, and took them prisoners. In Schwytz [?] and Unterwalden the division was more strongly marked. In Unterwalden (where was the scene) the men [?] divided and fought against each other, some joining the French from Stanz [?] to Engelberg. They were for freedom, and fought as the cause deserved. They killed 5000

French, more than double their own number; women fought; they were in all 2100 Swiss. One maid in the ranks, when her comrades were obliged to retreat, seeing a cannon yet unfired, went with a rope-end and fired it, killing thirty [?] French. She was taken; a pardon was offered. She said, "I do not acknowledge any pardon; my action is not pardonable; a thief [one?] pardons, not a just man." They killed her with swords. The hundred men who came from the higher part of Schwytz, attempting to go to their relief, were through their own countrymen forced to cut their way and march by night; and, when in retreating they came to the other shore of Lucerne Lake, they had again to cut through their own countrymen to arrive at their homes, they refusing them permission to pass. The Austrians, for the help the higher Valaisians gave them, from sovereigns have made them subjects to the lower Valaisians. The curate came in again, with a description of the Simplon; sat an hour and a half, then left the book. When [he was] not here I have written the part of my Journal I missed at the time, and the extract from his book. He came in again about 6 with a basket of prunes for me, and offered to go with me half-way, as he had to go to a church on the way.

September 26.—Got up at 5. The curate came, and, my foot being better, I set off. He showed me the bridge over the Massa where was a battle, and the ruins of a tyrant's tower. We came to his church, where he showed me the miraculous figure that was found in the Rhone. He told me the lower Valaisians were ready to join the French in '13, and that, in spite of this, they [the Austrians?] had given them a majority of voices. Left me in sight of Brieg, telling me he hoped to see me again in heaven. I walked on to Brieg; breakfasted, and then set off along the Simplon, a magnificent road indeed. It is cut in many places through the rocks, in others built up to its side. It has caverns and bridges always wide enough for four carriages; it ascends all the way to the new Hospice, and again descends from it. At its side are houses of refuge (as they are called) where many are kept by government, with privilege of selling food to help the passers-by. There is in each a room with a bed where one can go in case of rain, accident, etc.; and, when the time for avalanches etc., these men are obliged to accompany the travellers from house to house. Just where the rising ends the new Hospital was to have been erected, and is half done, but stopped now. A little farther on is the old one; whither I went, and got a dinner in the cell of one of the monks; bread, wine, cold meat, and nuts. He seemed very *ennuyé*; his words slowly fell; said they were St. Augustines, not St. Bernardites. That St. Bernard was a mere reformer of the order. They have been here since 1810 only, in an old castle for which they pay £20 a year. The Simplon was a department of France, and rather well off on account of the quantity of work and money, and not having the *droits* revenues. The Archduke Regnier was there a few days ago incog., and they did not recognize him—which mortified them very much. It is six leagues hither from Brieg, so that I had walked twenty-six miles.

I set off at 2: passed through Sempeln[?], and through the most magnificent scenery, through the granite galleries. The Italian part is by far the most difficult and splendid. The first boy that I met before coming to Isella, in answer to a question in German, answered "Non capisco";[20] I could have hugged. I arrived after much difficulty at Isella, knocked up. I was ruined in my feet, and it was not till near here that the carriages which parted in the morning from Brieg overtook me. Went to bed immediately in a room where the grease might be scraped from the floor.

September 27.—Did not get up till 1 on account of fatigue. Breakfasted most miserably, everything being bad; and then set off, but immensely slowly till a cart overtook me. Entered; lay upon the logs of wood and hay, and was driven to Domo d'Ossola. Is it imagination only that I find the sky finer, the country where cultivated extremely rich, green-looking? The dress of the women picturesque, blue with red stripes here and there; the men more acute and quicker-eyed. Arrived at Domo d'Ossola at 3; got into a clean though poor inn, and dined well. A gendarme came in to ask how it was that my passport had not been viséd yet; and then, seeing I was a physician, requested a cure for his toothache. It is useless to describe the picturesque: the best page to turn to for it is the memory. After one of the most comfortable fireside-evenings I have had since I left Geneva I went to bed at 7-1/2.

September 28.—Set off at 6 o'clock through vine-country, with little hills here and there starting out of the low Alps, highly cultivated, with beautiful little white villas at their tops and sides. Asked a woman what was a house whereon was painted a Democritus, Diogenes, etc. Answered, "È roba antica"[21]— though evidently modern, but deserted. Indeed, the whole of the houses seem too large for the inhabitants—much falling to ruin. From Domo d'Ossola went to Vella; to Vagagna, where I breakfasted and saw the first good-looking Italian girl. The children are pretty, the women quite otherwise. There began to suffer from my feet so much as that to go about six more miles took me five hours. No car passed me, or anything.

I arrived at last at Ornavasco. Could get no car, though they kept me half-an-hour in the yard standing, in hopes of getting one. At last agreed with a man that he should set off at 4 o'clock to-morrow to Fariolo for 4 francs. Looked at a bedroom: shrugged up my shoulders, but forced. Dinner: no meat, because "meagre." Ate the fruit. The Italian grapes, nectarines, peaches, and pears, I got yesterday, excellent. Two bunches of grapes half-a-franc: two at dinner.

Sunday, September 29.—Up at 5. Got into the char, or rather cart. Passed through Gravellino to Fariolo. Asked 10 francs to take me to Laveno: offered 4—accepted. Got into the boat. Rowed towards Isola Madre; passed Isola Pescatori; and landed on Isola Bella.

Went over the palace. Many of the floors miserable on account of their being the mere rock. Some good pictures. A whole set of rooms below in the style of grottoes, with windows looking on to beautiful views, close to the lake for *il fresco*. Looked at the terrace: not pleasing the style: and, thinking I should see it all in going round, did not go over the gardens. Went round the island in the boat; magnificently paved, like terrace on terrace.

Thence towards Laveno, intending to go to Lugano and Como; but, hearing that I could go all the way by water to Milan, I preferred this, and accordingly turned round towards Belgirato. Breakfasted on*caffè al latte, uve, and fichi,*[22] 4-1/2 francs. Boatman proposed my joining a party to Sestri-Calende, which I did. Arona, with the colossus, on my left, Anghera on my right; Monte Rosa; all the bottom part of the lake richly magnificent.

[The colossus is the celebrated gigantic statue of San Carlo Borromeo.]

Arrived at an inn—taken for a servant. After some time things got round, when in came two soldiers with swords by their sides, to desire me to step to the police-inspector. I did, and found he could not read the writing in my passport. The boatman came soon after, offering me a plan for to-morrow for five francs, and showing me twelve naps. they got for the boat—which cost only seventy francs. Agreed.

September 30.—Up at 5. Off at 6 in a large barge, with yesterday's English party and two carriages, by the Tessino and canal to Milan: at first through a fine hilly country, and rapidly by the Tessino flood. After, slower, and through a flat plain with trees and neat villas and hanging grapes, to Milan. Slept out of the town by the canal.

October 1.—Up at 7.

[Polidori blunderingly calls this "September 31": he also calls the day a Monday, but October 1, 1816, was a Tuesday. For the next following day he rightly writes "October 2."]

The boatman came as I had desired, to guide me. Entered Milan by a fine gate with a kind of triumphal arch. The streets are clean but narrow—fine houses. There are two strips of pavement for wheels, and often two for pedestrians. Passed by Santa Maria—fine, all white marble, with many fine statues on the outside. Many palaces. A bad taste shown in plastering the columns and corner-stones of a lighter colour than the body.

Got a letter from Brelaz; well written in composition and in letters, but badly spelled. Got my trunk, after some difficulty, passed. The diligence-keepers asked if they could direct me to rooms: showed two where a man was at that moment going. Got them for 40 lire il mese; a bedroom and sitting-room, second storey, Contrado San Spirito. Sent to the custom-house. Made the men wait—sent them away for two hours, again away for one. More stoppages, and, in centimes, 3 francs to pay. They would not at first let it (the trunk) go because it was the last day of the month.

[Did they share Polidori's blunder that the day was September 31?]

Went to dine at a restaurateur's: 1-1/2-franc dinner. Afterwards put my things into a little order, dressed, and went strolling towards Teatro della Scala. Entered, two hours before beginning, alone. Immense theatre: six rows of boxes, with, I think, thirty-six in a row. *La Testa di Bronzo*, a ballet, and a comic ballet: the ballet the most magnificent thing I ever saw—splendid indeed.

October 2.—Got up at 8. Breakfasted on grapes, bread and butter, wine, and figs. Wrote to Lord Byron. Dressed. Went to Marchese Lapone—out of town; Monsignor Brema—not at home. Walked about looking at booksellers' shops. Entered the Duomo—invisible almost, so black and dark. They were putting up drapery for Friday, which is the Emperor's birthday (probably the same as for Napoleon). Returned home, arranged my papers. Took a walk on the Corso; then to the Teatro Rè. The same price for all the places. The piece *Il Sogno di Ariosto* [Dream of Ariosto], where Fortune, Merit, Orgoglio, with Mrs. Disinganno,[23] were all personified. The dialogue abounded in truths, especially regarding women, which they applauded. The theatre is very small, like the Haymarket. Home to bed.

October 3.—Up at 8. Went to a circulating library: read Denina, *Vicende*, all the part on Italy and preface. To the Teatro Scelto di Milano. Enquired about Andricini etc. for my father—not found.

["Andricini" is clearly written in the transcript before me. I am not aware that there is any such Italian author as Andricini, and apprehend that the name ought to be Andreini. This author wrote, early in the seventeenth century, a dramatic poem entitled *Adamo*, which was indisputably present to Milton's mind when he was writing *Paradise Lost*. Dr. Polidori's father, who translated Milton, was probably interested in this work of Andreini.]

Went to the Teatro Rè;[24] a play of English people in which they kiss the hand, and make more bows than were ever made in a century in England. There were German soldiers in English uniforms present. Home, to bed.

October 4.—Up at 8—breakfasted. Went to call on Monsignore Brême—found him. Received me with two kisses and great apparent joy. About to learn English: I promised my help. Walked with me, and invited me to his box.

[Lord Byron, in two of his letters, October and November 1816, remarks regarding Milan: "The society is very oddly carried on—at the theatre, and the theatre only, which answers to our opera. People meet there as at a rout, but in very small circles.... They have private boxes, where they play at cards, or talk, or anything else; but, except at the cassino, there are no open houses or balls etc. etc."]

Left him—came home. Read Denina's *Ultime Vicende*, a poor book. Went to Guyler. Met Caravella—walked with him. Went to dine: where I met his brother, who told me the physician at Florence was dead, and promised to come and take me to the hospital. Met after dinner Abate Berlezi the Crabule.[25] Came home. Read the *Calandra* of Bibiena, and *Sofonisba* of Trissino. Took an ice, and went to La Scala. Feast of St. Francis, the Emperor's. When the Dukes went this morning to mass at the Duomo not a hat moved, not a voice of applause: however, when Regnier entered, there was a slight clapping of hands. The theatre was lighted up like an English one, and was magnificent, but showed what the Italians allege—that the scene does not improve by it, but the contrary.

In Brema's loge there were Monti, Brema's brother, and others. Monti a short man, round face, quick eye; pleasant in conversation, not haughty, modest, unassuming; seemed to take great pleasure in parts of the music and in the dancing.

[It will be understood that this is the celebrated Vincenzo Monti, the poet who was at one time acclaimed as the legitimate successor of Dante in virtue of his poem *La Basvigliana*, upon a personage of the French Revolution. In 1816 Monti was sixty-two years of age: he died in 1828. Though sufficiently Italian in his tone of mind and sentiment, he was not a consistent Italian patriot, but was eminently susceptible of inflation by a series of conflicting winds—anti-revolution, revolution, Napoleonism, and even Austrianism. Not indeed that he was sordidly self-interested in his various gyrations. As Dr. Richard Garnett has said: "He was no interpreter of his age, but a faithful mirror of its successive phases, and endowed with the rare gift of sublimity to a degree scarcely equalled by any contemporary except Goethe, Byron, and Shelley."]

Brema related that a friend of his, Porro, asked for a passport to Rome: refused, and asked for documents to prove his business. Gave what proved he had business at Maurata and relatives at Rome. Refused. Went to Swarrow, who told him he could not give it. Porro said: "Why do the Austrians think the Italians are always making conspiracies?" Swarrow said that they did not know, but, now that they had the upper hand, they cared not; and at last that, if Porro would give his word of honour not to visit any of the foreign embassies, he should have a passport. He had it. Porro was not a revolutionist but had always been against Napoleon, and had belonged to a legislative body by him dissolved on account of obstinacy. Brema and others accompanied me as far as the door, and I went to bed.

[It appears in the sequel that there were two Austrian governors in Milan at this period—Swarrow and Bubna—one for civil and the other for military affairs.]

From that day I neglected my Journal till this day,
December 8.—My residence at Milan lasted till October 30. During that time I had a most happy and pleasant life, Monsignor de Brême taking great friendship for me. My friends and acquaintance were Brême, Borsieri, Guasco, Cavalier Brême, Beyle, Negri, Byron, Hobhouse, Finch, Caravellas, Locatelli, Monti, Monti's son-in-law, Lord Cowper, Lord Jersey, etc.; Lloyd, Lee, Wotheron.

[Beyle was the great romance-writer best known as De Stendhal. In 1816 he was aged thirty-three, and had published only one book, entitled *Lettres écrites de Vienne sur Haydn, suivies d'une Vie de Mozart, etc.* He had seen some service under Napoleon, in Russia and elsewhere. His passionate admiration of the now dethroned Emperor induced him to retire from France towards 1814, and he resided in Milan up to 1821. He died in Paris in 1842.—Hobhouse had rejoined Byron in mid-September, and they had continued together since then.—Colonel Finch was the person through whom Shelley, in 1821, heard of the death of John Keats.—The Lord Cowper living in 1816 was the fifth Earl, born in 1778, and was married to a daughter of the first Viscount Melbourne.—The Earl of Jersey, born in 1773, was married to a daughter of the Earl of Westmorland.—Mr. Wotheron is spoken of later on under the name "Werthern." Neither of these surnames has a very English aspect, and I cannot say which is correct.]

De Brême and I became very intimate, and I believe he is really a good friend. In the morning at 10 o'clock I went to him to help him in English, and towards the end he corrected my Italian translation of *Count Orlando*.[26] We afterwards met at his box every night in the theatre of La Scala. He gave a dinner to Lord Byron, at which were a good many or rather all my acquaintances—Monti, Finch, Hobhouse, two Brêmes, Borsieri, Guasco (translator of Sophocles), Negri (author of *Francesca of Rimini*, a play). The dinner was very elegant, and we were very merry, talking chiefly of literature, Castlereagh, Burghersh, etc. We got up immediately after dinner, and went to coffee;

thence most to the theatre. De Brême was Vicar Almoner under the French Government. A priest came to him to ask leave to confess; Brême, knowing the subject, refused. The Princess was put to move Beauharnais, who sent for Brême and in a very angry mood asked him why he had refused leave. B[rême] said that, as he was placed to give leave, he imagined it was that it might not be granted indiscriminately, that he could not in his conscience give it, but that he was not the chief, and the Almoner, being applied to, might grant it. B[eauharnais] asked why, saying that the Princess wished it, and it must be done. De B[rême] said he had undertaken the office under the idea that his conscience was to be his guide; if not, the office should be immediately vacant; that he put it to Beauharnais himself whether a man who was buried in the vilest dissoluteness was a proper person to be entrusted with the care of young women's minds. Beauharnais said, "Right, right; you shall hear no more of it." This, and another occasion of the same nature, were the only occasions in which he saw Beauharnais privately; he avoided the court, and did not seek preferment. He twice under that government refused a bishopric, and under the new government; giving me as a reason that it went against his conscience to inculcate what he did not believe, and to add power to those who gave them, as he would be expected to side with them. He is violently for the independence of Italy. Christianity he believes not, and gives (I think) a new argument why we should not be holden to believe it. Saul, who was contemporary, who beheld the miracles etc., did not believe till a miracle was operated upon *him*; we at this distance cannot believe with greater facility. He has published an eulogium of Caluro, *Ingiustizia del Giudizio, etc.*, poems, etc. Has written several tragedies; *Ina* made me weep like a child. He is warm in his affections, and has never recovered the death of one he loved—a young noble lady, of great accomplishments and beauty. His friendship for me was warm: it gratifies me more than any attentions, friendship, or any relation I had before, with my fellow-companions. I cannot express what I feel for him. When parting from him, I wept like a child in his arms. He maintains from principle, not from belief, all the hardships imposed upon him by his tonsure. He would have the world to see that his belief is not swayed by a wish to escape from the bonds of the clerical state. He is charitable, giving away great sums of money in charity; eats only once a day, and studies all day till the hour of the theatre; kind to all who are recommended to him; sacrificing whole days to show them what he has seen a thousand times; a great admirer of English women; has an excellent library, of which I had the use. A great friend of comic, good-natured mimicry. Has an idea of writing *Ida*, a novel containing a picture of the most promising movements of the Milan revolution, and I have promised to translate it. He has two brothers; his father lives yet; his eldest brother is Ambassador at Munich. The youngest is Cavalier Brême—been officer in Spain; extremely pleasant and affectionate with me. Brême was a great friend of Caluro's, and to him Caluro dedicated one of his opuscules.

Borsieri, a man of great mental digestive power and memory, superficially read; author of *Il Giorno*, a work written with great grace and lightness. He was very intimate with me, Guasco, and Brême. Guasco, a Piedmontese; little reading, but great mental vision and talents. He also was one who attached himself a good deal to me. De Beyle, formerly Intendant des Marchés (I think) to Buonaparte, and his secretary when in the country. A fat lascivious man. A great deal of anecdote about Buonaparte: calls him an *inimitable et bon despote*. He related many anecdotes—I don't remember them: amongst other things, he said Buonaparte despised the Italians much.

[This last detail is confirmed in Beyle's *Reminiscences of Napoleon*, published not long ago.]

These four were the usual attendants at De Brême's box.

Monti is a short, roundish, quick-eyed, and rather rascally-faced man, affable, easily fired; talks rather nonsense when off poetry, and even upon that not good. Great imagination; very weak. Republican always in conversation with us; but in the first month, after having declaimed strongly in B[rême']s box about liberty and Germans, just as they were going out he said, "But now let us talk no more of this, on account of my pension." Under the French government he gained a great deal by his various offices; by this one he has been abridged of half. He translated the *Iliad* of Homer without knowing a word of Greek; he had it translated by his friends, word for word written under the Greek. Easily influenced by the opinions of others; in fact, a complete weathercock. He married the daughter of Pickler, the engraver; a fine woman, and they say an exceedingly good reciter, as he is himself. She has acted in his plays upon the Philodramatic stage. His daughter is married.

Negri—Marchese Negri[27]—a Genoese, not an improvisatore—very chatty; has at Genoa a most beautiful garden which all the English visit. Related to me Gianni's beginning. Gianni was an apprentice to a stay-maker, when one day an Abate, going into the shop, found him busily engaged in reading. Looking at the book, he asked him if he understood it. He said yes, and, on reading, showed it by his expression. The Abate, who was an improvisatore, asked him to see him next morning; when he improvised before him, and observed that the young Gianni seemed as if his mind was full and wished to give forth. He had him sent to school, and introduced him. Gianni in the Revolution, taking the Liberal side, was obliged to leave Rome, and, going to Genoa, Negri heard by letter of it, and went to seek him, inviting him to dine with him. He refused; and Negri, who had promised his friends that he would be of the party, at the hour of dinner went and found him with his nightcap on, deeply reading his favourite Dante; and in a manner dragged him by force to his house, where Gianni pleased much—and stayed a year at Negri's house, teaching him the art of improvisation. Gianni's improvisations were (many) improvised on the spot by an Abate into Latin verse.—Negri came to Brême's box several times, and had the effect of making all except Brême burst with laughter: me he sent to sleep.

Lord Byron came to Milan, and I saw him there a good deal. He received me kindly, and corrected the English of my essay in *The Pamphleteer*.[28] He visited a good deal Brême's box. Mr. Hobhouse was with him.

Colonel Finch, an extremely pleasant, good-natured, well-informed, clever gentleman; spoke Italian extremely well, and was very well read in Italian literature. A ward of his gave a masquerade in London upon her[29] coming of age. She gave to each a character in the reign of Queen Elizabeth to support, without the knowledge of each other, and received them in a saloon in proper style as Queen Elizabeth. He mentioned to me that Nelli had written a Life of Galileo extremely fair, which, if he had money by him, he would buy that it might be published,—in Italy they dare not; and that Galileo's MSS. were in dispute, so that the heirs will not part with them; they contain some new and some various readings. Finch is a great admirer of architecture and Italy.—Wotheron, Mr., a gentleman most peaceable and quiet I ever saw, accompanying Finch; whose only occupation is, when he arrives at a town or other place, to set about sketching and then colouring, so that he has perhaps the most complete collection of sketches of his tour possible. He invited me (taking me for an Italian), in case I went to England, to see him; and, hearing I was English, he pressed me much more.—Locatelli was the physician of the hospital, a good unimpostoring physician. I saw under him a case of pemphizus, and had under my care an hysterical woman.

Jersey, Lady, promised to enquire of her mother, Lady Westmorland, if she would employ me as her physician; but said she thought my having been with Lord B[yron] a great objection.

[I have an impression, not a secure one, that Dr. Polidori did act to some extent as Lady Westmorland's medical adviser. It would here appear that her Ladyship was not very partial to Byron; and Byron must have repaid her dislike, for I find, in a letter of his to Murray, November 1817, that Polidori was in the way of receiving "the patronage of Frederic North, the most illustrious humbug of his age and country, and the blessing of Lady Westmorland, William Ward's mad woman." Joseph Severn the painter (Keats's friend), who saw a good deal of Lady Westmorland at one time, terms her "this impulsive, arrogant, dictatorial, but witty and brilliant woman."]

Lloyd;—as I was moving in the pit, found him, and never saw a person so glad in my life. He offered me half of the money he had at his banker's, as he thought I must be much embarrassed. Told meBrelaz and Bertolini seemed to be together, and that the man seemed worked off his legs.

My life at Milan was very methodical. I got up, went to the hospital, breakfasted, came home, studied, dined, and then at 7 went to the theatre. Between breakfast and study went to de Brême to help him in English. It was proposed too, by him, to teach English, which I had intended to do.

I saw only the dome under which is the chapel of St. Borromeo—very rich in silver, crystal, and jewels. The body is vested in pontificals, and quite dry. The orbits seem only filled with a little heap of black dirt, and the skull etc. is black. There is here the gnometer of Cassini. They preserve here a nail of the cross of Christ.—St. Ambrose, the ancient Cathedral. It was at the gates of this that Theodosius was refused entrance.—The Brera library; and the Ambrosian, where I saw the Virgil with marginal notes of Petrarch; some of the pieces of MSS. of the Plautus and Terence, fragments edited by Mai.—Some of the paintings there are beautiful. The Milanese Raphael has some heads expressing such mild heavenly meekness as is scarcely imagined.

[This Raphael is, as many readers will know, the *Sposalizio*, or Espousal of the Virgin Mary and Joseph. Being an early work by the master, it exhibits, in its "mild heavenly meekness," more of the style of Perugino than of that which became distinctive of Raphael in his maturity.]

When at Milan, I spent almost all my money in books, buying nearly 300 volumes, not being able to resist that thirst for printed sheets, many of which I never shall read.

Swarrow, the Governor of Milan, when the Emperor was there, accompanying him to the theatre, saw that one poor man in the pit, leaning against a box, had dared to keep his hat on. Violently enraged, he enters the box, without leave or saying a word; and, leaning over the box with all his orders dangling at his breast, applies two hearty slaps to the poor man's cheeks, and then, rising majestically, leaves the box, and goes to receive the despot's smile. This making a great hubbub, and exciting a great deal of ridicule against the noble police-officer, he insisted with the police-director that not a word more should be allowed to be said.

When at Milan, there came Sgricci, a Tuscan, under the patronage of Monti, who puffed him most egregiously, especially his tragic *improvisati*. I accompanied de Brême to Casa Crivelli, where I saw Swarrow and a cardinal; a dried-up ganache[?] with a face of malice that had dried up with the features of the face, but still remained sketched there in pretty forcible lines. The improvisator entered; yellow boots with trousers, blue coat, and a Flemish collar to his shirt. He began *The Loves of Psyche and Cupid*; commonplace, unpoetic rhymes. *Coriolanus*, a tragedy; such an abominable opiate that, in spite of my pinching myself and Cavalier Brême rousing me every minute, I found myself, when ended, roused by the applause from a pleasant nap. Heard him again at the theatre; terza rima; *The Grief of Mausolea*. [30] The only bearable parts were those about Aurora, night, etc., which he had beforehand prepared, to clap-in at convenience, from the *Gradus ad Parnassum*. The tragedy being drawn out, first came *The Death of Socrates*. He came forward, saying that, this subject being undramatizable, he would, if the public insisted, attempt it, but that he had rather another might be drawn. *Montezuma* came out. "Oh," says he, "this will touch your passions too much, and offend many probably personally." The public here stoutly hissed, and insisted he should proceed; he as stoutly called on the boy to draw, which he did, and, there coming forth *Eteocles and Polynices*, he was satisfied, making *olla podrida scenica* of French ragouts, Italian minestras, and Greek black soup. It was reported that Monti's taking him up was by the persuasion of his daughter. An epigram was written upon Sgricci, as follows nearly—

"In questi tempi senza onore e merto
Lavora Sgricci in vano, ha un altro il serto."

[The translation of this couplet is—"In these times without honour and merit Sgricci labours in vain—another man wears the wreath." It will be seen that the epigram, if such it can be considered, runs in favour of Sgricci. He was a native of Arezzo, and, as our text shows, a renowned improvisatore. I happen to possess a printed tragedy of his, *Ettore*, which is notified as having been improvised in the Teatro Carignano, Turin, on June 13, 1823. Shelley in January 1821 attended one of Sgricci's improvisations, and was deeply impressed by it as a wonderful effort, and even, considered in itself, a fine poetic success. In 1869, being entrusted with some MS. books by Shelley through the courtesy of his son the late Baronet, I read a tribute of some length which the great English poet had paid to the Italian improvisatore: it has not yet been published, and is included, I suppose, among the Shelley MSS. bequeathed to the Bodleian Library. The subject on which Shelley heard Sgricci improvise was Hector (Ettore). One rather suspects that the *Ettore* improvised in 1823 may have been partly reminiscent of its predecessor in 1821. The portrait of Sgricci, a man of some thirty-five years of age, appears in the book which I possess: it shows a costume of the fancy-kind that Polidori speaks of. I have looked through the tragedy, and do not concur in the tone of ridicule in which Polidori indulges. An improvise can only be criticized as an improvise, and this appears to me a very fair specimen.—As I have had occasion here to re-mention Shelley, I may as well add that Medwin (*Life of Shelley*, vol. i, p. 250), says that the poet had no animosity against Polidori, consequent upon any past collisions: "Shelley I have often heard speak of Polidori, but without any feeling of ill-will."]

Going one evening with L[ord] B[yron] and Mr. H[obhouse] to B[rême]'s box, Mr. Hobhouse, Borsieri, and myself, went into the pit, standing to look at the ballet. An officer in a great-coat came and placed himself completely before me with his grenadier's hat on. I remarked it to my companions: "Guarda a colui colla sua berretta in testa" (I believe those were my words), waiting a few minutes to see if he would move. I touched him, and said, "Vorrebbe farmi la grazia di levarsi il cappello purch'io vegga?" He turning said "Lo vorreste?" with a smile of insult. I answered: "Sì, lo voglio."[31] He then asked me if I would go out with him. I, thinking he meant for a duel, said, "Yes, with pleasure"; and called Mr. Hobhouse to accompany me. He did. When passing by the guard-house he said, "Go in, go in there"; I said I would not, that it was not there I thought of going with him. Then he swore in German, and drew half his sabre with a threatening look, but Hobhouse held his hand. The police on guard came, and he delivered me to their custody. I entered the guard-house, and he began declaiming about the insult to one like him. I said I was his equal, and, being in the theatre, to any one there. "Equal to me?" he retorted; "you are not equal to the last of the Austrian soldiers in the house"; and then began abusing me in all the Billingsgate German he was master of—which I did not know till afterwards. In the meanwhile the news had spread in the theatre, and reached de Brême and L[ord] Byron, who came running down, and tried to get me away, but could not on any plea. De Brême heard the secretary of police say to the officer: "Don't you meddle with this, leave it to me." De Brême said he would go to Bubna immediately, and get an order for my dismission; on which the officer took Lord Byron's card, as bail that I would appear to answer for my conduct on the morrow. Then I was released.

Next morning I received a printed order from the police to attend. As soon as I saw the order I went to De Brême, who accompanied me to the gate. I entered.

"Where do you wish your passport viséd for?"

"I am not thinking of going."

"You must be off in four-and-twenty hours for Florence."

"But I wish for more time."

"You must be off in that time, or you will have something disagreeable happen to you."

Brême, upon hearing this, immediately set off to Bubna, and I to Lord Byron, who sent Mr. Hobhouse in company of Colonel McSomething to Swarrow to ask that I might not be obliged to go. They went. Swarrow received them with a pen in his hand; said it was a bagatelle; that the Secretary of Police had been there in the morning, and that he had told him of it. That it was nothing, that I should find myself as well off in any other city as there, and that, if I stayed, something worse might happen. Hobhouse tried to speak. S[warrow] advanced a foot; "Give my compliments to Lord Byron; am sorry I was not at home when he called." "But if this is so mere a trifle ..."—"I hope Lord Byron is well"; advancing another foot, and then little by little got them so near the door that they saw it was useless, and left him. De Brême in the meanwhile had been to Bubna. Bubna received him very politely, and said he had already seen Colonel M., who had explained to him the whole; and that for the mistake of speaking to the officer on guard he thought it enough that I had been put under arrest. "I am much obliged to you, and am glad then that my friend will not have to leave Milan." "What do you mean?" Brême explained. "It is impossible, there must be some mistake, for I have had no memorial of it. I will see Swarrow this evening about it." De Brême mentioned with what idea I had left the theatre. Bubna said that German soldiers had one prejudice less; and at the theatre in the evening I heard many instances of the officers of the Austrian Army acting meanly in this respect. Amongst others, Bubna's son, being challenged for insulting a lady at a public ball, accepted the challenge, but said there were several things he had to settle first, and that he would appoint a day for the following week. He left Milan the Saturday before. A young Italian had a dispute with a Hussar officer, and challenged him, for which he was brought before the police and reprimanded. Some days after, the officer, standing at a coffee-room door, asked him if he wished to settle the affair with him. He said yes, and they immediately entered. The officer spoke to several of his companions in the room, and they all struck the young man, and pushed him out. He could get no redress.

[This affair of Dr. Polidori's shindy in the theatre excited some remark. His feelings in favour of Italy and Italians were keen, as he was himself half Italian by blood; and he was evidently not disinclined to pick a quarrel with an Austrian military man. He was indiscreet, and indeed wrong, in asking an Austrian officer on guard to take off his cap; and, although he addressed the officer at first in courteous terms, his expression "Lo voglio" was not to be brooked even by a civilian. Lord Byron mentioned the matter in a letter to his sister, November 6, 1816, as follows: "Dr. Polidori, whom I parted with before I left Geneva (not for any great harm, but because he was always in squabbles, and had no sort of conduct), contrived at Milan, which he reached before me, to get into a quarrel with an Austrian, and to be ordered out of the city by the Government. I did not even see his adventure, nor had anything to do with it, except getting him out of arrest, and trying to get him altogether out of the scrape." And on the same day to Thomas Moore. "On arriving at Milan I found this gentleman in very good society, where he prospered for some weeks; but at length, in the theatre, he quarrelled with an Austrian officer, and was sent out by the Government in twenty-four hours. I could not prevent his being sent off; which, indeed, he partly deserved, being quite in the wrong, and having begun a row for row's sake. He is not a bad fellow, but young and hot-headed, and more likely to incur diseases than to cure them." Beyle likewise has left an account of the affair, translated thus. "One evening, in the middle of a philosophical argument on the principle of utility, Silvio Pellico, a delightful poet, came in breathless haste to apprise Lord Byron that his friend and physician Polidori had been arrested. We instantly ran to the guard-house. It turned out that Polidori had fancied himself incommoded in the pit by the fur cap of the officer on guard, and had requested him to take it off, alleging that it impeded his view of the stage. The poet Monti had accompanied us, and, to the number of fifteen or twenty, we surrounded the prisoner. Every one spoke at once. Polidori was beside himself with passion, and his face red as a burning coal. Byron, though he too was in a violent rage, was on the contrary pale as ashes. His patrician blood boiled as he reflected on the slight consideration in which he was held. The Austrian officer ran from the guard-house to call his men, who seized their arms that had been piled on the outside. Monti's idea was excellent: 'Sortiamo tutti—restino solamente i titolati' (Let us all go out— only the men of title to remain). De Brême remained, with the Marquis di Sartirana, his brother, Count Confalonieri, and Lord Byron. These gentlemen having written their names and titles, the list was handed to the officer on guard, who instantly forgot the insult offered to his fur cap, and allowed Polidori to leave the guard-house. In the evening, however, the Doctor received an order to quit Milan within twenty-four hours. Foaming with rage, he swore that he would one day return and bestow manual castigation on the Governor who had treated him with so little respect."—One other observation of Beyle, regarding Polidori and Byron, may be introduced here. "Polidori informed us that Byron often composed a hundred verses in the course of the morning. On his return from the theatre in the evening, still under the charm of the music to which he had listened, he would take up his papers, and reduce his hundred verses to five-and-twenty or thirty. He often sat up all night in the ardour of composition."—As Polidori's passport is prominently mentioned at this point of the Diary, I may add a few particulars about it. It was granted on April 17, 1816, by the Conte Ambrogio Cesare San Martino d'Aglia, Minister of the King of Sardinia in London; and it authorized Polidori to travel in Italy—no mention being made of Switzerland, nor yet of Lord Byron. The latest visa on the passport is at Pisa, for going to Florence. This is signed "Il Governatore, Viviani," whom we may safely assume to have been a relative of Shelley's Emilia. The date of this final visa is February 17, 1817.]

October 30.—Got up early next morning, packed up my books and things; then went to seek for a coach that was parting for Lodi. Found one, and fixed that a vetturino, who was going to set off next day for Florence, should take me up at Lodi. Went to see de Brême. He told me he had been to Bubna's, but that he had found him out at a council of war, and that he had left an order none should follow him. I took leave of de Brême, and wept in his arms like a child, for his kindness and friendship had been dear to me. I took leave of L[ord] B[yron], H[obhouse], and Guasco. The last offered me his services in any way, and said he should take it as a favour the oftener he was applied to. I got into the coach with only 5 louis in my pocket, leaving my books in the care of de Brême, and left Milan with rage and grief so struggling in my breast that tears often started in my eyes, and all I could think of was revenge against Swarrow and the officer in particular, and a hope that before I left Italy there might be a rising to which I might join myself. I arrived at Lodi; wrote to Lloyd to ask him to lend me some money, and went to bed exhausted.

October 31.—Up at 9: breakfasted. Went to see the Duomo and other churches without feeling interest; the hospital, which is a magnificent building. Returning to the inn, I met the vetturino. I found in the coach a Prussian student of Heidelberg who had made the campaigns of '13 and '14 with the rest of his companions, and who was banished Heidelberg for slapping a Russian in the face. Growled against his king for not keeping his promise; hated the French, and gave me an interesting account of the way of spending the winter evenings in his part of Germany, Pomerania; the young working at some pursuit of hand, the old relating their tale of youth. A Milanese woman and son. We went that evening to Casal Panterlungo. Supped and went to bed, I and the Prussian in the same room.

November 2.—Up at 4. Across the Taro to Parma. Went, in spite of my having so little money, in search of books—Boccaccio's *Fiammetta*. The Cathedral and Baptistery. From Parma to Reggio, a beautiful town with fine palaces and porticoes, though, on account of the few inhabitants, appearing a huge sepulchre. To Rubiera: supped and slept.

November 3.—Up at 4. Through Modena, where I saw the Duomo, and the Tower which contains the Lecchia porticoes—palaces of the Duke—four orders heaped one on the other. Here they examined my box, and were going to send it to the dogana on account of books; when, upon my saying I was a physician, they let them pass.

At Bologna supped with the Prussian. To the opera. Saw a ballet, extremely ridiculous: barbarian dances with astonishing powers of limbs forming in the air [postures] out and in on their feet.

November 4.—Up at 9. Went to see the churches and (a) private gallery. After dinner roamed about the town in a most melancholy mood, entering the churches and sitting in the dark for an hour, etc. Went to the Theatre of Cento Cavalli: beautiful Greek architecture. To bed—a play.

November 5.—At 10, expecting to have been called before, the vetturino came, saying he would not go, since I had hindered the Prussian from setting off on Monday, without security; and that he would go to the police to gain it from the Prussian that he should be paid at Florence. After a good deal of disputing I gave it, in a promissory note that I would pay if he could not. Found afterwards it was only to get time.

Went to see the churches, the public place, San Prospero, the Neptune. After dinner to Madonna Santa Lucia. Along the portico "Questo è da vendere"[32] was written on portions of the wall. The public cemetery. Saw a coffin, when dark, brought into the church with torches. The poor are separated from the rich, and have only the turf upon them: the rich groan under the weight of marble. The priests, monks, nuns, etc., all in separate squares; a cardinal's hat covering a death's head.

Returned to Bologna. Went to the theatre. Saw *Agnese*: wept like a child: the acting of the madman inimitable. Went to bed.

November 6.—Up at 11. Set off with the Prussian and an Italian officer across the Apennines. Oxen in continual use. Misty, so could not enjoy the view. Dreadful winds to Pianoro. That evening the officer related all the services he had been in; French liberty, Consulship, Emperor. Refused by the Austrians; went to Murat, and now going to offer himself to the Pope; if not accepted, to America. For which side? "Spanish or Creole."[33] He had the unfeelingness to joke upon his father's being killed in the time of the liberty-rows, saying he got that for not changing; on which I felt so nettled that I spoke for half-an-hour upon the ruin the fickleness of the Italians had brought upon themselves. He felt, I think, ashamed; at least he gave up that kind of light talk.

Forgot to say that at Modena I presented[34] my passport so that the "24 hours" were invisible; and left at Modena one who had accompanied us from Piacenza, telling the most barefaced lies about boars, dogs, and thieves, that were ever heard.

November 7.—At 4 up. Arrived at night at Fortebuona. Dreadful wind and rain. Supped and went to bed.

November 8.—At 5 walked a good part of the road. Arrived at Florence by the Porta San Gallo, through the Arch. The custom-house officer, when we told him, if he wanted to look, he might open, [replied]: "Che? Un servo del sovrano? Ci sono dei facchini."[35]

Florence, on entering, disappointed me, as we were obliged to go round on account of the road being mended. Went to the inn. Dressed—not having changed linen since Milan. Went to the post: no letters. In despair, remaining with only four scudi. Walked about the town,—Arno: into the Cathedral and Baptistery.

Went to seek Cavalier Pontelli.[36] Knocked at his door, along Arno—both before and behind. Could not make any one hear. One who lived near (Lecchini), upon my asking how to get in, said he was thankful to say he was not Pontelli, and did not know. Returned home. Gave the Prussian a missal I had bought at Bologna. He broke my pipe. Went to bed. Wrote to Pontelli and Brême.

November 9.—Got up; went to seek Pontelli. Found he had a villa at Porta San Gallo. Went thither, knocked; saw his head pop out of the window in a greasy night-cap. On my announcing myself, he descended, opened the door, and received me with welcome. Found him at breakfast, sausages, caviare, etc. Sat down; told me his housekeeper would not show herself; invited me to come to his house instead of the inn. Went into town; took a peep at the Gallery—at the precious vases, Venus, etc. Went to the inn. Put up my things, paid; and, seeing the Prussian envied me my desk, I gave it him, on condition that, if we ever met again, he would paint me a picture he sketched in my album. Went to Pontelli; dined; accompanied him to town. His servant took a porter to carry my things to the Arno house, and then we went to pay visits.

In the way he told me he lived very retired, and very economically that he might not want; that the people now looked upon him with a good eye; that the Government also did not prosecute him; and that he in fine thought that a revolution would be general—trying to persuade me that his avarice was mere policy.

Went to pay a visit to Cavalier Tomasi, a Cortonian. Found many in the room, who all sat upon me about English politics. Left them when they were going to play. Thence to Abate Fontani, Librarian of the Riccardi Library. Talked of Madame de Staël, Finch, etc.

Returned home. Found I was in the house of the Capponis, Pontelli having the lower storey.

November 10.—Up at 9. Dressed in black silk etc., the housekeeper going to mass; and, Pontelli apparently not being willing that I should accompany her, I went out a little after, and went to the same church, where I spoke with her. Looked at the church; and then went to San Lorenzo, Santo Spirito [Santa

Croce],[37] where I saw the tomb of Galileo, Machiavelli, Alfieri, Cosmo de' Medici, etc.

Returned, and went with a letter from de Brême to the Countess of Albany. Found there several. Presented my letter: "Very like your father."

[The Countess of Albany, it need hardly be said, was the widow of Prince Charles Edward Stuart, the "Young Pretender." Born in 1752, Princess of Stolberg-Gedern, she married the Prince in 1772. Being much ill-treated by him, she left him, and maintained a practically conjugal relation with Conte Vittorio Alfieri, the famous dramatic poet: they could have married after a while, but no nuptial ceremony took place. Alfieri died in 1803, and the Countess then became very intimate with a French painter, much younger than herself, named Fabre. She died in Florence in January 1824. If Dr. Polidori had been a Jacobite, he would have held that, in waiting upon the Countess of Albany, he was in the presence of the Queen Dowager of the United Kingdom of Great Britain and Ireland. It will be observed that the Countess told Polidori that he was "very like his father." The latter had, from 1787 to 1789, been secretary to the Conte Alfieri, and had known the Countess in Colmar and Paris. In one of his privately printed books he has left on record a little anecdote of the royal dame, which, trifling as it is, may find a place here. "While the Conte Alfieri was slowly recovering health I was invited to pass the evenings with him and the Countess, so that on various occasions I '*fui terzo tra cotanto senno.*'[38] But this honour did not last long. For one time when I was with them the lady turned her eyes on me, and asked Alfieri why my thighs were rounded while his were flat. 'Stuff and nonsense,' he replied, wrinkling his nose, and he passed on to some different talk. From that time I no more had the honour of being one of the exalted party; neither could I complain of this, for I myself felt that that question had been unseemly, and more in character for a drab than for a discreet and modest lady."]

Conversation became general. Republics being brought upon

the tapis, I took to defending them, especially against a gentleman near me. After some time he went, and I gathered he was brother to the King of Prussia.

Took my leave, and came to dinner, after going to the caffè to wait for Pontelli. Rain hindered him from keeping his appointment, so that I went at last alone to San Gallo, he having the custom of staying the Sundays only in town. Was presented by him to Lecchini, the Inspector of Police, who recognized me as a Tuscan, and the domiciliary communication was made out as such.

November 11.—Tried to stay at home. Forced by Pontelli's long-in-vain repeated hints to go out; jealous of his young housekeeper, though she is hardly worth it. Roamed about, dined, and went to bed.

November 12.—Same. Dined with him at a restaurateur's.

November 13.—Got up at 7; tired of Pontelli, and set off for Arezzo, with a shirt in my pocket and with my dog. When at Incisa it began to rain; walked on through Feline, Monte Varchi, to Arezzo. Thunder and lightning excessive, with violent rain. I was at last so numbed that when roused I seemed to be wakened; my dog could not stand it, but at 7 miles from Arezzo fell. I did not perceive it, but walked on. Arrived at 8, having walked 45 miles in 12 hours, having stopped once at Incisa to eat and rest. Found my uncle's house; knocked. The servant, hearing I was his nephew, flew up-stairs, and I met a tall, stout, slovenly woman, my aunt. On the second storey, where they lodged, they made a fire. I changed my things for my uncle's, and while changing he arrived—a tall, stout, handsome, mild-looking man. Put myself to bed; ate, and they left me to sleep.

[This uncle, Luigi Polidori, was a physician, and had a considerable reputation for the cure of the local typhoid fever (tifo).]

November 14.—Found myself well; no cold, only my left groin stiff from a wound in my foot. Saw my two cousins, Pippo and Teresa; put myself to study. After 6 went with my uncle to Signor

Gori, where I heard music. Four or five girls wanting husbands, two priests, whitewashed walls, and several young men, were the entertainment.

While at Arezzo, my life was quiet enough; study till I went out at 6, when I went to play at cards and talk at Signor Gori's. Saw the prisons. One of the descendants of a true Lombard family walking about in a dirty sailor-looking jacket. Signora Onesti and daughter the most abominable scandal-talkers I ever heard, though she was a Pitti. Library always shut. The School of Ignatius a fine building. Churches fine: the Chapel of St. Mary, the Cathedral with the basso-rilievo altars, the church with the altar painted by Vasari, etc.—I recovered my dog.

November 21.—Set off to return to Florence with half-a-scudo in my pocket; having refused to accept from my uncle, not being willing to let him know how it stood. Frost on the ground: hurt my foot. Lost my dog again at Montesarchi. At Feline got into a carriage, not being able to do more on account of my foot. Met a physician, a cavaliere and his wife. Arrived at 7; Pontelli lent me a scudo to pay.

November 22, 23, 24.—Stayed at Pontelli's on account of my foot, though Pontelli tried to send me out under pretence that I should see the town. But, not being able, he stayed at home till 6, when he told me I had better go to bed—which I generally did to quiet him. No letters according to servant.

November 25.—Tired of Pontelli. That I might go to Pisa, I issued out intending to sell my watch-chain; but as a last chance looked at the Post Office, and found two letters from Lloyd, who, as soon as he had received my letter, set off from Venice to see me. On the road he lost his purse with 36 louis, and, having no letters at Florence, he could only give me 20 scudi. Received me with great kindness, and assured me that, while he had money, I should never want. Dined with him and Somers. They advised me to settle in Florence as physician to the English. I however determined to see Vaccà first; wished him good-bye, as he was obliged to go to Rome for money.

[There were two brothers named Vaccà, or Vaccà Berlinghieri, who had been known to Gaetano Polidori in Pisa before he left Italy with Alfieri. Gaetano (who was a native of Bientina near Pisa, his family belonging chiefly to Pontedera) also stayed in the same house with the Vaccàs in Paris after leaving his secretaryship with the Count. They were then both medical students. One of them, Leopoldo—who had been intimate with Napoleon while the latter was in the Military College—abandoned medicine, and served under the French empire in Spain, dying not many years afterwards. The other brother, Andrea, attained an European reputation in medicine, and especially surgery: Shelley, when in Pisa, consulted him more than once.]

November 26.—Went to seek the Naviglio, to go by water to Pisa. At going out, stopped by the gate-officer, who, on hearing me enquire where the boat was, would not let me pass without proofs of my being *originario Toscano*; so I went to Lecchini, and got him to write me a declaration. The boat could not set off to-day, so returned to Pontelli and went to bed.

November 27.—At 7 set off in the boat on the Arno for Pisa.

November 29, 30, December 1.—Stayed in my room, copying *Osteologia* of my grandfather.

[This *Osteologia* is a treatise on osteology written in verse—octave stanzas. The author was Agostino Ansano Polidori, by profession a surgeon, born in 1714 and deceased in 1778. In 1847 Gaetano Polidori printed this poem at his private press. He had previously made a MS. copy of it, with an introduction giving a few family-particulars. One statement made in this introduction is that the mother of Agostino was a Florentine lady named Folchi—"perhaps" (so says Gaetano Polidori) "descended from an English family domiciled in Florence, which may have changed its name Folks into Folchi."]

December 2.—Up at 9; went to see Vaccà; still at hospital. While waiting for him, saw an Austrian colonel, who, in the excess of his gratitude to Vaccà, called him the *Dio della Medicina*. Vaccà expressed great joy to see me; told me to make his house my own;

to dine there when I chose, and often; to begin to-day; not to use ceremony. Left me, and I returned home; went to dine at V[accà]'s. Introduced me to his wife, a pleasing pretty Frenchwoman, the former wife of his brother; he had just obtained the Pope's dispensation to marry her. Spent the evening there.

December 3, 4, to 21.—Went to the hospital in the mornings when Vaccà was not ill; three or four times to the Library. Studied in the mornings; went to dine either at Vaccà's or at eating-house; always evenings at Vaccà's. Corsi, a well-informed lawyer, cav[alier] serv[ente] to V[accà?];[39] Mario ex cav[alier] serv[ente]. Cecco Castanelli, Pachiani, etc.; chess with the English; with Vaccà. For the various information I obtained there see notes.

[The Pachiani (or Pacchiani) here mentioned must certainly be the same Abate Pachiani who in 1820 introduced Shelley to the Contessina Emilia Viviani, to whom the poet dedicated his *Epipsychidion*. Medwin, in his *Life of Shelley*, a book which does not now obtain many readers, gives a lively but partly very unfavourable account of Pachiani: I append a few extracts from it, more as being relevant to Shelley than to Polidori. "Pachiani was about fifty years of age, somewhat above the common height, with a figure bony and angular. His face was dark as that of a Moor. During the reign of Austrian despotism he was admirably calculated for a spy. As to his religion, it was about on a par with that of l'Abate Casti. At Pisa, il Signore Professore was the title by which he was generally known. He lost [his professorship] by an irresistible *bon mot*. During one of his midnight orgies, which he was in the habit of celebrating with some of the most dissolute of the students, he was interrogated, in the darkness, by the patrole in the streets of Pisa as to who and what he was,—to which questioning he gave the following reply: 'Son un uomo pubblico, in una strada pubblica, con una donna pubblica.' His epigrams were *sanglants*, and he gave sobriquets the most happy for those who offended him. His talent was conversation—a conversation full of repartee and sparkling with wit; and his information (he was a man of profound erudition, vast memory, and first-rate talent) made him almost oracular. He was a mezzano, cicerone, conoscitore, dilettante, and I might add ruffiano."[40]]

December 21.—Went in the evening to the Countess Mastrani's. Ices, iced people, prepared poetry, music. Went to the theatre, in the days past, several times. Saw Goldoni's *Bugiardo*, with Harlequin etc.

December 22.—As usual.

December 23.—Same.

December 24.—Ditto.

December 25.—Christmas-day. Walked along Arno. Spent the evening and dined at Vaccà's.

December 26.—Up at 7. Went with Vaccà to Leghorn, a neat, regular, well-built town. The first thing I went in search of was the sea, and I stood gazing some time on the waves. The Public Place and Strada Maestra fine. Saw Vescali's collection of alabasters. Returned by 3. Dined with Vaccà. Went to the theatre with Mrs. Vaccà, who introduced me to Signora Bettina Franciuoli.

December 27.—As usual. Up at 4—dined at Vaccà's—went to theatre, and to B.'s box.

December 28.—Went to hear nella Chiesa dei Cavalieri (after a ride with Mrs. Vaccà) Nicolini play a sonata upon the organ, which is perhaps the finest in Italy. There were the Prince Villafranca, the Countess Castelfiel, Princess della Pace, and other nobles. At Vaccà's and theatre.

December 29.—Up at 3-1/2. Dined at Vaccà's: theatre. English etc. as usual.

December 30.—Up at 1. Reading Sismondi. Got up—went to Vaccà to dine. After English, to the Casa Mastrani: all evening with Sofia. The others—Biribro, Dionigi.

[According to a letter from Lord Byron, April 11, 1817, Dr. Polidori had at least three patients at Pisa—Francis Horner, a child of Thomas Hope, and Francis North, Lord Guilford. They all died—which may or may not have been partly the Doctor's fault.]

With this entry we come to the end of Dr. Polidori's Diary—although (as I have before intimated) not by any means to the end of his sojourn in Italy. He saw Byron again in April 1817 in Venice: Shelley, to the best of my knowledge, he never re-beheld.

I add here two letters which Polidori wrote to his sister Frances (my mother, then a girl of only sixteen), and two to his father. The first letter was written soon after beginning the journey with Byron; the last not long after the date of parting from him. I also add a letter sent to Mr. Hobhouse during Polidori's sojourn with Byron, and a note, of much later date, written by Mrs. Shelley to my father, Gabriele Rossetti.

The letter to Mr. Hobhouse, it will be observed, goes over some of the same details which appear in the Diary. This letter has been copied by me from the Broughton Papers, in the Manuscript Department of the British Museum (Add. MSS. 36456 to 36483). I did my best to trace whether these papers contain anything else relating to Polidori, and I do not think they do. In fact, the affairs of Lord Byron, and the very name of him, scarcely figure in those Broughton Papers at all: for instance, I could not find anything relating to his death.

JOHN POLIDORI TO FRANCES POLIDORI.

MY DEAR FANNY,

I shall see Waterloo in a day or two—don't you wish to be with me? but there are many more things that I have seen which would have given you as much pleasure. Shakespear's Cliff at Dover, the French coast, the phosphorescent sea, Bruges, Ghent, Antwerp, and Brussels, have all got more than is in any of Feinaigh's plates to excite the memory to bring forth its hidden stores. The people amongst whom we are at present dwelling is one that has much distinguished itself in the noblest career, the race for liberty; but that tends little to the ennobling of a people without the sun of literature also deigns to shine upon them.

It was not the warlike deeds, the noble actions, of the Greeks and Romans or modern Italians, that has rescued these names from the effacing daub of oblivion; if it had not been for their poets, their historians, their philosophers, their heroes would in vain have struggled for fame. Their actions would have been recorded in the dusty legends of monks, and consequently have been forgotten, like those of the Belgians, Carthaginians, and others. How many fine actions of modern times will be buried in oblivion from the same want, and how many merely secondary characters will be handed down with a halo round their deeds reflected from the pages of historic genius!

I am very pleased with Lord Byron. I am with him on the footing of an equal, everything alike: at present here we have a suite of rooms between us. I have my sitting-room at one end, he at the other. He has not shown any passion; though we have had nothing but a series of mishaps that have put *me* out of temper though they have not ruffled his. The carriage, the new carriage, has had three stoppages. We are at present at Brussels merely to have the carriage-part well looked at and repaired.

The country till here has been one continued flat; and, except within this neighbourhood, we have not seen a rising ground on which to feast our eyes. Long avenues paved in the middle form the continued appearance of our roads. The towns are magnificently old, such as England cannot rival, and the state of cultivation is much greater than in England: indeed we have not seen a weed or a foot of waste ground all our way. The people in the country show no misery; the cottages comfortable, whitewashed, large-windowed, shining with brass utensils internally, and only having as many heaps of dirt as there are inhabitants—who certainly throw away all their cleanliness upon the house, fields, roads, and windows. But I will not fill my letter with this, as some time you will either see my Journal in writing or print—Murray having offered me 500 guineas for it through Lord Byron. L[ord] B[yron] is going to give me the manuscript, when done printing, of his new cantos of *Childe Harold*.[41]

Have you seen Mrs. Soane and Mr. S[oane]? how are they? If you see them, remember me to her and him. I shall write when I have seen the seat of *his* hero's glory, *mine's* disgrace; no, not disgrace—misfortune. See Mrs. S[oane], and write how she is.

How are you all at home? Papa, Mamma, Meggy (have you heard from her?), Charlotte, Bob, Henry, Eliza, and Mr. Deagostini. Remember me to all, and to all who enquire about me not merely from curiosity—telling me in your next whether they exceed the number 0. I am very well, and wrote Mamma from Ostend.

I remain, my dear Fanny,

Your affect. Brother,

J. POLIDORI.

Brussels, *May 2, 1816.*

Write to me—Dr. Polidori, à Genève, poste restante,—and soon, as I shall be there in 12 days.

To JOHN HOBHOUSE, WHITTON PARK,
near HOUNSLOW.

Coblentz, *May 11, 1816.*

DEAR SIR,

As we are at last some way on our journey, I take a sheet of paper up, in despair of filling it, to tell you we are both well and hearty. Lord Byron's health is greatly improved, his stomach returning rapidly to its natural state. Exercise and peace of mind, making great advances towards the amendment of his *corps délabré*, leave little for medicine to patch up. His spirits, I think, are also much improved. He blithely carols through the day, 'Here's to you, Tom Brown': and, when he has done, says, 'That's as well as Hobhouse does it.' You and his other friend, Scrope Davies, form a great subject of conversation.

143

God! here I am at the end of all my thoughts. Oh no! Waterloo was ridden over by my Lord on a Cossack horse, accompanied by myself on a Flemish steed; Lord Byron singing Turkish or Arnaout riding-tunes, and your h[umble] s[ervant] listening. We had a very good day of it. Lord Byron visited Howard's (I think, Colonel) burying-place twice. We have had two days by preëminence in our tour—to-day and Waterloo. To-day we came from Bonn hither through the finest scenes I ever saw, modern and ancient; the 13th and 18th century forming an *olla podrida* with the bases given in the year 1. Towers and towns and castles and cots were sprinkled on the side of a.... But here I am on poetic stilts, cut short for prose ones.

They boast—the Ministerialists and others—of ours being the happy land. I should like to carry John Bull to Flanders and the Rhine: happiness, content, cleanliness (here and there), husbandry, plenty without luxury, are here bestowed on all. War has had no effect upon the fields; and even at Waterloo no one (except for the glittering button or less brilliant cuirass in beggar's hand) would imagine two such myriaded armies had met there. No sulkiness is seen upon the face here, and no impudence. On the Rhine and in Flanders there are hardly any beggars. To-day we had nosegays given us by little girls for centimes. But the other day, coming to Battice, we met the best beggars: three little girls, pretty though not well dressed, ran along our carriage, crying out—"Donnez-nous un sou, Monsieur le Général en chef"; and another, "Chef de bataillon." Having given these some, a boy followed, pulling faces comic enough to make such grave dons laugh, and crying out, "Vivent Messieurs les Rois des Hanovériens—donnez-moi un sou."

As I fear I have tried your eyes, and lost my pains after all on account of the illegibility of my accursed pen's scratches, I must end—assuring you at the same time I am with esteem

Yours etc.,

THE DIARY OF
DR. JOHN WILLIAM POLIDORI

J. Polidori.

We count upon being at Geneva in ten days at best. Excuse the bad writing etc., for I am in a fever of digestion after my ride.—J. P.

To Gaetano Polidori.

September 20, 1816.

My dear Father,

You judged right with regard to my writing. I had written twice since your letter announcing *The Pamphleteer*, and was anxiously waiting yours. Your letter gave me pleasure; and I was indeed in want of some just then, for I was in agitation for my parting from Lord Byron. We have parted, finding that our tempers did not agree. He proposed it, and it was settled. There was no immediate cause, but a continued series of slight quarrels. I believe the fault, if any, has been on my part; I am not accustomed to have a master, and therefore my conduct was not free and easy. I found on settling accounts that I had 70 napoleons; I therefore determined to walk over Italy, and (seeing the medical establishments) see if there proves a good opportunity to settle myself, so that I hope I am still off your hands for nine months: perhaps Lady Westmorland, who is at Rome, is desirous of having an English physician for longer, I having a letter for her from Mme. de Staël. I shall write to-day to Vaccà and Zio [uncle] for letters to Milan to physicians, in your name; and at present, till I think they and my trunks can have arrived, will wander amongst the Alps,—in which course I am now at Thun, almost in the centre. I have seen Mont Blanc and its glaciers, and will see the Jungfrau, Grindelwald, and Grimsel. Then I will go by the Simplon to Milan, whither direct to me poste-restante, only putting my Giovanni etc. names in full, as there are Polidoris there.[42] I am in good health and spirits; I hope this won't hurt yours, for assure yourself I will do all I can not to allow you to feel any inconvenience on my account.

Remember me to my mother, who I know will feel deeply this disappointment; to Mary,[43] Fanny, and Charlotte, to Signor Deagostini and Signor De Ocheda, and to all.

If you could get me letters of introduction, they would be of great use. In the meanwhile, my dear father, believe me

Your affectionate son,

JOHN POLIDORI.

JOHN POLIDORI TO GAETANO POLIDORI—TRANSLATION.

Arezzo, *November 14, 1816.*

DEAR FATHER,

I fear you must be in much anxiety at not having heard from me for so long; but the reason was that I did not wish to write before having seen my uncle—to whom I went the day before yesterday, and who received me with great affection and pleasure. I wrote to him from Thun. Thence I went to Grindelwald and Lauterbrunner; thence to Interlachen, and, by the Lake of Brientz, to Meyringen; by the Grimsel in the Valais to Obergasteln; thence to Brieg; and then by the Simplon down to Farinoli in the Borromean Islands. Thence I embarked to Sestri Calende; thence to Milan—where, meeting the poet Monti, Lord Byron, Monsignor de Brême, and others of my acquaintance, I remained some weeks. Thence I went to Florence, by Bologna, Modena, Parma, and Piacenza, and crossing the Apennines. In Florence I stayed two days, and saw Cavalier Pontelli, Abate Fontani, Dr. Frosini, and others. Thence I went on foot to Arezzo, where I found my uncle, my aunt, Pippo, and Teresa, all well; and they received me with great cordiality into their house, where I now am.

Seeing, by your letter to my uncle, in how much trouble you

are on my account, I have determined, after learning whether Lady Westmorland will employ me or no—if yes, to go to Rome; if no, to go straight from Leghorn to London, to the bosom of my family. I shall soon hear from Lady Westmorland, as Lady Jersey undertook, at the instance of Monsignor de Brême, to ask her mother whether she wants me or not, and she is now in Florence, *en route* for Rome. In case she should tell me yes, I shall at once go to Rome: but meanwhile I don't proceed any farther than Arezzo. If she says no, I shall be off to Leghorn, and return to London.

I wish that in your next letter you would send me enough money, in a bill on Florence, for paying the passage from Leghorn to London, for the chance of my not having enough remaining....

When I see you again I shall have much to tell you about, but will not put it into a letter. Suffice it that I have found that what you told me about Italy is but too true. I am in good health....

Your affectionate son,

JOHN POLIDORI.

[To this letter the uncle Luigi Polidori added something. One point regarding Lord Byron is of a certain interest.]

I became indignant at some references [made by John Polidori] to the strange conduct of that Lord with whom he was travelling: but *he* kept his temper well—I envy him for that. All these people are hard: Sævus enim ferme sensus communis in illâ fortunâ.—Patience!

* * * * *

[My father, about the date of this ensuing letter, met Mrs. Shelley several times, and he liked her well. He did not think her good-looking: indeed I have heard him say "Era brutta" (she was ugly).—The letter is written in fairly idiomatic, but by no means faultless, Italian.—I am not aware whether Gaetano Polidori supplied Mrs. Shelley with information, such as she asked for,

for her Biography of Alfieri: perhaps a minute inspection of the book might show.—*Cleopatra*, acted in 1775, was Alfieri's first attempt at tragedy.]

Harrow, *April 20, 1835*.

Courteous Signor Rossetti,

Thank you so much for your amiable reply, and the interest you show in the undertaking of a pen but too unworthy of those great names which give so much lustre to your country. Meanwhile I am about to make a farther request: but am afraid of showing myself troublesome, and beg you to tell me your opinion sincerely. I should not like to seem to take impertinent liberties; and, if my idea appears to you impracticable, don't say anything about it to any one.

I am informed that your Father-in-law the celebrated Polidori can relate many interesting circumstances regarding Alfieri. The Life which I am writing will be printed in *Dr. Lardner's Cyclopædia*: therefore it is very short, running perhaps to 70 pages—not more. Thus, if I could introduce some details not yet known but worthy of publication, I should be very pleased indeed. I don't know whether Polidori would be willing to give me such details. For example, I should like to know whether Alfieri was really so melancholy and taciturn as is said by Sir John Hobhouse in his work, *Illustrations to the Fourth Canto of Childe Harold*; whether he gave signs of attachment to his friends, and whether he was warmly loved by them in return. Some anecdotes would be welcomed by me; also some information about the Countess of Albany. There is an affectation of silence, as to all that relates to her, in whatever has yet been written concerning Alfieri. But, now that she is dead, this is no longer necessary. Were they married? If not, nothing need be said about it; but, if they were, it would be well to affirm as much.

I shall be in London next Sunday, and shall be staying there several days. But I am in a quarter so distant from yours (7 Upper Eaton Street, Grosvenor Place) that it would be indiscreet to ask for a visit from you—and much more indiscreet to say that, if Signor Polidori would visit me, he could perhaps tell me some little things more easily than by writing. As the Tuscans say, "Lascio far a lei."[44] You will do whatever is most fitting, and will give me a reply at your convenience.

Repeating the thanks so much due to your kindness, believe me

Your much obliged servant,

M. W. P. SHELLEY.

I hear that Alfieri was intimate with Guiccioli of Ravenna, the latter being then quite young; and they had a joint idea and project (which did not turn out manageable) of establishing a national theatre in Italy. Possibly Signor Polidori knows about this. Is there any historical work containing particulars about the closing years of the royal husband of the Countess of Albany? I don't know, and am in the dark. He (is it not so?) was the last of the Stuarts, except his brother the Cardinal of York.

Oh what trouble I am giving you to reply! Really I now feel more than ashamed of it. But you are so kind. And, besides, the grammar of this letter must be like Alfieri's *Cleopatra*.

FOOTNOTES:

1. The word, as written by Charlotte Polidori, seems to be "dole" rather than anything else. It looks as if she had copied the form of Dr. Polidori's word without understanding what it was. I substitute "door," but this is done *faute de mieux*.
2. Such is the word written by Charlotte Polidori. I fancy it ought to be "late."
3. Only an initial is written, "M": but I suppose "Master"— *i.e.* Michael Wohlgemuth—is meant.
4. It seems rather odd that Polidori should make this jotting, "and (not) towns." Perhaps he aimed to controvert the phrase, "scattered cities crowning these," in Byron's poem quoted further on.
5. These are the precise words as they stand in Charlotte Polidori's transcript. It is to be presumed that Dr. Polidori wrote them some while after May 13, 1816.
6. I don't understand "Mayor" in this context: should it be "Mylor"?
7. No name is given: should it be Shelley? Another Englishman who was in this locality towards the same date was Robert Southey.
8. I don't think there was any such stone-pelting in Geneva: it took place elsewhere in Switzerland.
9. The word written is perpanism, or possibly perhanism. Is there any such word, medical or other? Should it perchance be pyrrhonism?
10. The "ghost-story" which Polidori *published* was *The Vampyre*: see p. 128 as to his having begun in the first instance some different story.
11. Word obscurely written.
12. "Blind" appears to be the word written. It seems an odd expression—meaning, I suppose, "to blind (mislead or puzzle) the auditors."
13. This, again, is not clear to me: something in the nature of a game of forfeits may be indicated.
14. So written: should it be "Bingwen" or something of the kind?

15. The word "society" is perfectly clear in Charlotte Polidori's transcript. From the context, I question whether it ought not to be "Shakespear." As to "the criticism of Johnson" on Gray in the *Lives of the Poets,* many of my readers will recollect that this criticism is somewhat adverse, Gray being treated as a rather nebulous writer.
16. Seems rather an odd phrase, but I suppose correctly transcribed.
17. A name is written here, but so obscurely that I leave it out. It somewhat resembles "Neravois," or "the ravois."
18. Should this be "glaciers"?
19. This name is illegibly written: I can only suppose that it must be meant for Brieg.
20. "I don't understand."
21. "It's an old affair."
22. Coffee with milk, grapes, and figs.
23. Orgoglio is pride; disinganno is undeceiving, disillusion.
24. There is a word following "Rè," evidently the title of the play which was acted. It looks something like "Amondre," but cannot be read.
25. The word is more like Crabule than anything else: I don't understand it.
26. Presumably some English book, but I know not what.
27. I think the name would correctly be Marchese di Negro: my father had some correspondence, towards 1850, with the then Marchese of that family.
28. This essay was on the Punishment of Death.
29. The word written is "his"; but the context shows that this must be a mistake.
30. *i.e.* Artemisia, who built the mausoleum of Halicarnassus.
31. The speeches run thus: (*a*) Look at that man, with his cap on his head. (*b*) Would you do me the favour of taking off your hat, so that I may see? (*c*) Would you wish for it? (*d*) Yes, I wish it. In Italian, this last phrase has an imperative tone, "I will it."—It may be added that the Austrian's phrase "Lo vorreste?" was itself not civil: the civil form would have been "Lo vorrebbe ella?"

32. "To be sold."
33. These words form (I *suppose*) the answer of the Italian officer—
    i.e. he would side with either party indifferently.
34. I presume that the word should be "presented": the writing looks
    like "pented."
35. "What? A servant of the sovereign? There are porters."
36. I suppose that Pontelli was a person who had been more or less
    known to Dr. Polidori's father before the latter left Italy in 1787,
    and that the father had given his son some letter of introduction
    or the like. Or possibly the introduction came from some
    acquaintance in Geneva or in Milan.
37. The name of Santa Croce is not in the MS.: but it ought to be,
    as this is the church containing the sepulchral monuments of
    Galileo, etc.
38. "Was third amid so much intellect." The phrase is adapted from
    a line in Dante's *Inferno*.
39. Rather (it must be understood) to *Signora* Vaccà.
40. Ruffiano does not correspond to our word "ruffian," but to
    "pimp" or "go-between."
41. No doubt this intention was not carried into effect.
42. These Polidoris were not (so far as I know) members of the same
    family as John Polidori.
43. This was Dr. Polidori's elder sister, Maria Margaret, who in my
    time was invariably called "Margaret" in the family.
44. "I leave the question to you."

Transcriber's Note

The original spelling and punctuation have been retained.

Variations in hyphenation and compound words have
    been preserved.